SVEN B. F. JANSSON is Professor of
Runology at the Royal Academy of Letters,
History and Antiquities in Stockholm.

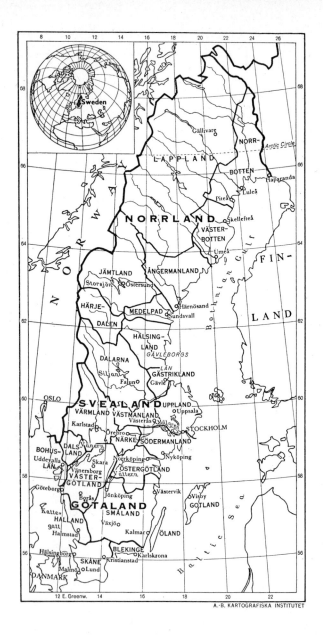

A.-B. KARTOGRAFISKA INSTITUTET

THE RUNES OF SWEDEN

By SVEN B. F. JANSSON

TRANSLATED BY PETER G. FOOTE

THE BEDMINSTER PRESS NEW YORK 1962

Most of the pictures in this book have been
taken for "The Runic Inscriptions of Sweden",
published by the Royal Academy of Letters,
History and Antiquities. The photographers
were: Iwar Anderson, Marianne Bratt,
Harald Faith-Ell and Nils Lagergren.

Library of Congress Catalog Card Number 62-9692

© *Sven B. F. Jansson 1962*
Printed in Sweden 1962 by
Kungl. Boktryckeriet P. A. Norstedt & Söner, Stockholm

CONTENTS

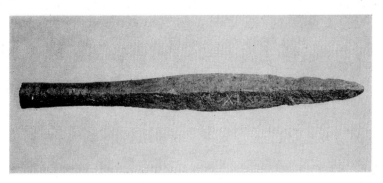

Plate 1. The spearhead from Mos, Gotland

THE OLDEST INSCRIPTIONS OF SWEDEN

More than 3000 runic inscriptions are known from Sweden — nearly four times as many as are known from the rest of the Germanic world put together.

Not least because of this wealth of material, the runic inscriptions make an important contribution to our knowledge of the culture and society of ancient Sweden. They are Sweden's oldest linguistic monuments and they give us much contemporary information of inestimable value. The inscriptions often enable us to draw significant conclusions for the general history of culture.

The oldest known runic inscription from Sweden is found on a spearhead, recovered from a grave at Mos in the parish of Stenkyrka in Gotland. The inscription, consisting of only five runes, might be

5

dated to the end of the third century of our era. Its appearance on a weapon is typical, for it is on objects such as shield-mounts, spearheads, personal ornaments and household articles that the oldest inscriptions occur.

The Mos inscription may be read as *gaois* (or as *sioag*), but what was meant by this is impossible to say. Perhaps it is the spear's name, or part of its name. Uncertainty of interpretation is also quite typical of the oldest, so-called Primitive Norse, inscriptions, made in the first centuries of our reckoning. Most of the extant inscriptions from this time cannot, in fact, be interpreted, and probably never will be with any certainty. This is one reason why these oldest inscriptions are given such summary treatment here, although they deserve a detailed study, both for their own sake and because of the great interest they arouse from other points of view. But in such a survey as this it is sufficient to mention two more inscriptions of this truly archaic type: the Kylver stone and the Möjbro stone. These two represent entirely different kinds of Primitive Norse inscriptions. In contrast with the Mos inscription they are cut in stone — the material in which the great majority of the inscriptions are preserved. (Inscriptions in less durable material, in wood for example, have with few exceptions crumbled away and perished for ever.)

Like the Mos spearhead, the Kylver stone comes from Gotland. The inscription, which is usually dated to the end of the fourth or beginning of the fifth

6

Plate 2. The Kylver Stone, Gotland

century, chiefly consists of the Primitive Norse runic alphabet, the symbols appearing in the characteristic runic order, unparalleled in any other known writing system. The fame of the Kylver stone depends on the fact that it is thus the oldest record we have of the Germanic runic series. The symbols, which are a little damaged here and there, may be reproduced thus:

fuþarkgwhnijpeRstbèmlngdo

Immediately after the last rune comes a sign which looks most like a simply-drawn firtree; and then higher up to the right of this are the five runes *sueus*.

The Kylver stone served as one of the slabs in a sarcophagus. Its location in a grave hidden under the ground gives us at once some inkling of what purpose the rune carver meant his inscription to serve. We are evidently dealing with magic and sorcery, as in so many of the earliest Norse inscrip-

7

tions. The Kylver stone was cut with runes in order to protect the grave and its occupant; or perhaps to bind the dead to his new home, to prevent his returning to upset and interfere with the lives of the living. To achieve the protection deemed necessary the rune carver has had recourse to three powerfully effective magical means: first, the runic alphabet itself, then the greatly reinforced *t*-rune (which is what the "firtree" is), and last the word of magic might, *sueus*, which, as befits its mysterious purpose, reads the same backwards as it does forwards.

Utterly different from this inscription made in the service of the powers of darkness is the imposing rune stone at Möjbro in the heart of the realm of the Swedes, raised about the year 500 to stand in full view of the people. It was set up in memory of *Frawaradar*, 'the resourceful', and it is perhaps a picture of him that appears on the stone, galloping his slack-reined horse. He holds his shield in his left hand and brandishes his weapon in his right. Two animals run beside the horse. The whole scene has a rare living quality, everything caught in motion. It seems as if this picture reveals the Migration Age's fruitful contact with the culture of Rome. Certainly at the time when the Möjbro stone was carved, a steady stream of Roman gold was flowing into the northern lands.

Memorial stones of about the same age as the Möjbro stone are also known from other parts of Sweden, but these have no pictures and in a number of cases the inscriptions contain only personal names.

Plate 3. The Möjbro Stone, Uppland

Like the Möjbro stone, the Rö stone in Bohuslän was probably raised in memory of a man killed in battle. The inscription, partly damaged where the surface has flaked, reads: "SwabaharjaR is treacherously slain (?). I StainawarijaR cut the runes. I HraRaR set up the stone . . .."

On some southern Swedish rune stones from about the middle of the seventh century onwards traces are apparent of the radical changes which runic writing and the Norse language underwent in the latter part of the Migration Age. One gets an impression of confusion and disintegration. But about A.D. 800, when the Viking Age begins, we find that a conscious reform of the system of runic writing has been made, apparent in the two variant forms of a new 16-symbol runic alphabet. This Viking Age runic alphabet is a greatly simplified writing method and, from a linguistic point of view, decidedly inferior to the old 24-symbol series. But it had practical advantages, not for the reader, it is true, but for the writer, who in many cases was spared the need for an accurate analysis of the sounds of the words he wished to represent.

There are comparatively few inscriptions from the period before the Viking Age; their language is often difficult to interpret and their message obscure. The first two centuries of the Viking Age (A.D. 800—1000) also have little material to offer, although on consideration it m ɹsnbe decided that this is because runes were then chiefly cut in wood or other material less durable than stone or metal. All that one can say is that in the ninth and tenth centuries memorial inscriptions were not cut on raised stones in any great numbers; but fortunately, with the advent of the eleventh century, this practice became fashionable in Sweden.

To this early part of the Viking Age, the ninth century, poor in inscribed stones as it otherwise is, belong nevertheless two of Sweden's most remarkable runic monuments: the Rök stone in Östergötland and the Sparlösa stone in Västergötland. The two stones are strikingly dissimilar. The Sparlösa stone is decorated with interesting pictures of an individual kind, which are as difficult to interpret as the runic inscription, unfortunately damaged in some important places; the Rök stone on the other hand is completely covered with runes, front, back, sides and top — no space has been given up to any other ornament.

The Rök stone is not only the most impressive monument ever raised in Sweden to commemorate a dead kinsman — it also stands as the great memorial of Swedish literature in antiquity. It is true that inscriptions in verse form are already to be found in the Migration Age, chiefly in the powerful language of sorcery, highly-wrought and archaically obscure, and it seems possible to glimpse a developed poetic art of magico-mythical character behind a number of Primitive Norse inscriptions. And later in the Viking Age we shall also meet rune carvers with some literary pretensions. But no inscription gives us such deep insight into the world

11

Plate 4. The Rök Stone (front), Östergötland

of ancient literature as does the Rök stone. Some of the inscription is obscure; it reads thus:

Aft Væmoð standa runaʀ þaʀ. Æn Varinn faði, faðiʀ aft faigian sunu.

Sagum mogminni(?) þat, hværiaʀ valrauðaʀ vaʀin tvaʀ þaʀ, svað tvalf sinnum vaʀin numnaʀ at valrauðu, baðaʀ saman a ymissum mannum.

Þat sagum annart, hvaʀ fur niu aldum an urði fiaru(?) meðr Hraiðgutum, auk do meðr hann umb sakaʀ.

> *Reð Þioðrikʀ*
> *hinn þurmoði,*
> *stilliʀ flutna,*
> *strandu Hraiðmaraʀ.*
> *Sitiʀ nu garuʀ*
> *a guta sinum,*
> *skialdi umb fatlaðʀ,*
> *skati Mæringa.*

Þat sagum tvalfta, hvar hæstʀ se Gunnaʀ etu vettvangi an, kunungaʀ tvaiʀ tigiʀ svað a liggia.

Þat sagum þrettaunda, hvariʀ tvaiʀ tigiʀ kunungaʀ satin at Siolundi fiagura vintur at fiagurum nampnum, burniʀ fiagurum brøðrum. Valkaʀ fim, Raðulfs syniʀ, Hraiðulfaʀ fim, Rugulfs syniʀ, Haislaʀ fim, Haruðs syniʀ, Gunnmundaʀ fim, Biarnaʀ syniʀ . . .

Sagum mogminni þat, hvaʀ Inguldinga vaʀi guldinn at kvanaʀ husli.

Sagum mogminni, hvaim se burinn niðʀ drængi. Vilinn es þat. Knua knatti iatun . . .

Sagum mogminni: Þorr. Sibbi viavari ol nirøðʀ.

"For Væmod stand these runes. And Varin wrote

them, the father for his dead son. I tell the ancient tale which the two war-booties were, twelve times taken as war-booty, both together from man to man. This I tell second who nine generations ago ... with the Reidgoths; and he died with them, because of his guilt.

> Theodric the bold,
> king of sea-warriors,
> ruled over
> Reid-sea shores.
> Now sits he armed
> on his Gothic horse,
> shield strapped,
> protector of Mærings.

This I tell in the twelfth instance where the horse of the Valkyrie sees food on the battle-field, where twenty kings lie. This I tell in the thirteenth instance, which twenty kings sat on Sjælland for four years, with four names, sons of four brothers: five called Valke, sons of Radulv, five Reidulvs, sons of Rugulv, five Haisls, sons of Harud, five Gunnmunds, sons of Björn ... I tell the tale which of the Ingvaldings was revenged through a wife's sacrifice. I tell the ancient tale to what young warrior a kinsman is born. Vilin it is. He could slay a giant ... I tell the ancient tale: Thor. Sibbi, guardian of the sanctuary, ninety years of age, begot a descendant."

This unique inscription appears to contain many allusions to heroic lays and legends now lost. It thus gives us an insight into the literature that flourished at the beginning of the Viking Age. But it is with sadness that the modern reader must admit that these allusions in their compressed form can call up no associations in his mind. The literary milieu in which Varin incised his runes is not to be recovered; the tales and poems that were well known in Öster-götland in the ninth century are, and doubtless always will be, wrapped in oblivion. And yet this cannot destroy the Rök stone's priceless value as a literary document.

The beginning of the inscription, with its allite-ration and solemn rhythm, gives at once the im-pression of an artistically mannered prose. Many poetic expressions occur in the text, and in some places the word order adopted is proper only to the elevated language of poetry.

A complete stanza is found in the middle of the inscription. It is striking what close associations this poem on *Þioðrikʀ* has with West Norse poetry, both in verse-form and in vocabulary and poetic idiom (see pp. 118—21, where the verse on Swedish rune stones is discussed).

The Sparlösa stone dates from about the same time as the Rök stone. In the inscription — still only understood in part — the reader is invited to interpret *runaʀ þaʀ ræginkundu*, "the runes derived from the divine powers". The same lofty adjective to describe runes is found on the Noleby stone in Västergötland (seventh century), whose original site seems to have been inside a grave: "Runes,

15

a   b

Plate 5. The Sparlösa Stone

derived from the gods, I cut . . ." This word, *regin-kunnr* in Old Icelandic, has otherwise only been found once, in the *Hávamál*, and there too it is used of runes:

> *Þat er þá reynt*
> *er þú at rúnum spyrr*
> *inum reginkunnum*
> *þeim er gørðu ginnregin*
> *ok fáði fimbulþulr . . .*

16

"Then it is proved, when you ask about the runes derived from the gods, those which the mighty powers made and the great word-master [= Odin] painted . . ."

Like other important cultural advances, the invention of runes was thus ascribed to divine intervention. It was the ancient Norse belief that Odin had discovered these mystic and mighty signs.

As mentioned before, the Migration Age and the early Viking Age have little runic material to offer, little in comparison with the eleventh century, at any rate. This latter century, which saw the end of the Viking Age and the transition from the ancient to the medieval world in Sweden, was a period of rare vitality and variety in Swedish history. Runic inscriptions in almost overwhelming numbers survive from this time, illustrating many aspects of eleventh-century life.

THE VIKING EXPEDITIONS

The great forays are generally felt to be the most typical expression of the Viking Age and the one that most catches the imagination. It is not inappropriate to begin with an account of what the rune stones can tell us of the Viking expeditions, for it was often precisely to commemorate kinsmen who

Plate 6. Head of a Viking carved in elk-horn. This little sculpture, which was found at Sigtuna in 1937, probably dates from the 11th century

had fallen in foreign lands that the stones were raised. When the great expeditions were over, the old trade routes closed and the Viking ships no longer made ready each spring for voyages to east and west, then that meant the end of the carving and setting up of rune stones in the proper sense of the word. They may be called the monuments of the Viking voyages, and the sensitive reader may catch in many of their inscriptions the Viking's love of adventure and daring exploits in defiance of wind and weather.

It should perhaps be emphasized that the Viking forays did not merely mean ferocious raids — they also had great importance as a realisation of commercial policy. In the Viking Age the Norsemen were the chief middlemen in the commercial traffic between the Orient and western Europe. For long periods the Scandinavian North was at the focal point of world trade — a fact which is at once evident from the enormous finds of English and Arabic coins that have come to light in Swedish soil.

ON THE EASTERN ROUTE

The expeditions eastward undoubtedly had the longest traditions behind them. There the Vikings followed routes that had long been explored. The oldest statement concerning a Swedish eastward expedition is to be found on the Kälvesten stone in Östergötland. The inscription, which can be dated to the ninth century, was carved in memory of Öjvind: "He fell eastwards with Ejvisl". The Viking expedition mentioned on this stone was to be followed by many others in the same direction. The Swedish rune stones of the eleventh century can tell us much about these eastward ventures. The foreign country whose name most often occurs on them is Greece, *Grikkland, i Grikkium*, a term that denotes the north-east Mediterranean lands of the Eastern Empire. It is clear that journeys there were especially frequent, and judging by the inscriptions this destination was found particularly enticing by men from the central Swedish districts. It is not of course to be expected that the brief runic texts should give any detailed account of adventures met with on the expeditions, but a number of them at any rate tell us something more than the bare fact that the man in

19

Plate 7. The boulder at Ed (front), Uppland

whose memory the stone was set up *varð dauðr i Grikkium* — "died amongst the Greeks".

On a huge boulder at Ed, just north of Stockholm, are found two handsome inscriptions. They face an ancient track that winds through the forest along the shore of Edssjön. The inscriptions read thus:

"Ragnvald had the runes cut in memory of Fastvi, his mother, Onäm's daughter. She died in Ed. God help her soul.

> Ragnvald let
> the runes be cut.
> He was in Greece,
> he was leader of the host."

This Ragnvald, whose name (see p. 83 below) shows him to have been a man of high birth, had thus by his own account been commander of a troop of warriors in Greece — *var a Grikklandi, vas liðs forungi*. All things considered, it seems most likely that the reference here is to that famous bodyguard of Norse mercenary soldiers, known as the Varangians, who were in the service of the Byzantine emperors at this time. One can readily appreciate Ragnvald's eagerness to announce to his contemporaries — and to posterity — that he had held the distinguished post of commander in the Varangian corps in 'Micklegard' — Constantinople.

The Varangian Guard was undoubtedly a well-known institution to those who took the road past the boulder at Ed. To many a young man it breathed an irresistible temptation to adventure.

That the voyages to Greece were frequent and on a large scale is also clearly shown by the fact that one of our provincial law-codes from medieval times still contains a special provision concerning men who were in Greece. Amongst the laws of inheritance it says: "He can receive no inheritance as long as he stays in Greece."

In the period when the Swedish Greek-stones were cut, there were livelier connections between Scandinavia and Byzantium than at any other time. Swedish Viking ships were then a common sight in the Black Sea, the Sea of Marmara, and the Ægean.

The Varangian corps came into existence at the end of the tenth century and by the beginning of

Plate 8. The Ulunda Stone, Uppland

the eleventh century this military élite among the units in the emperor's body-guard had won great fame. Ragnvald came home to Uppland and could himself tell of the honour he had gained in Byzantium. But most of the runic inscriptions are memorials to men who sailed away and never returned to their homeland.

At Ulunda ford (west Uppland) stand two rune stones, one on either side of the spot where the road crosses the stream. Like the boulder at Ed these stones thus stand by a road — and a much more important road than the bridle-path by Edssjön. The ford at Ulunda is on Eriksgata, the road, that is, by which a newly elected king had to travel through the country to be recognized by the people as their ruler. It is noteworthy how many rune stones were set up in the vicinity of this road, the most important highway in Sweden. (On rune stones erected *nær brautu*, 'near the road', see pp. 129—130 below.)

The inscription on one of the Ulunda stones, raised by Kår and Kabbe, ends with a verse; the heir honours the dead man in the following words:

For hæfila	"He went boldly,
feaʀ aflaði	wealth he gained,
ut i Grikkium	out in Grikkland,
arfa sinum.	for his heir."

One of the many Swedish runic monuments concerning men who travelled to Greece is now preserved in England. What happened was that in the seventeenth century the English embassy in Stockholm, on behalf of the English king, sought permission to export two Swedish rune stones to Oxford. Permission was granted by King Karl XI in

23

Plate 9. The Ed Stone. Now in Oxford

1687, and both stones joined the University's antiquarian collection. One of them is a typical Greekstone, with the inscription: "Torsten had this memorial raised after Sven, his father, and after Tore, his brother. They had gone out to Greece. And after Ingetora, his mother. Öpir cut [the runes]."

The father had evidently taken one of his two

sons with him on the expedition to Greece. Torsten doubtless had to stay at home to look after the farm with Ingetora, his mother. The family lived in Ed, where the rune stone originally stood — not far from the boulder by Edssjön described above. Sven and Tore and Torsten must often have read the inscription that told of Ragnvald's successful journey to Micklegard and his career with the Varangians. Their expedition was less fortunate. As the inscription shows, both father and son died out there.

It may be added that the English ambassador's choice of rune stones to send to Oxford might have been better considered. Would it not have been more appropriate if he had tried to obtain a couple of stones that told of viking forays to England? He would have had plenty to choose from. See pp. 49—60 below.

The travellers to Greece steered their ships east across the Baltic. By the great river-systems of *Garðaríki* (Russia) they made their way "to Greek harbours", as it says on the rune stone that Ljut the skipper raised in memory of one of his sons: ... *styrði knœrri, kvam hann Grikkhafniʀ* ... "He steered the ship, he came to Greek harbours".

There were several routes to choose from. Once the open waters of the Gulf of Finland were crossed, the ship could be brought by the channels of the river Neva in to Ladoga, where the trade-routes divided, one going in a southerly and one in an easterly direction. The usual route went by the river Volkov down to Old Ladoga, called Aldeigjuborg by the Norsemen. Then the travellers had arrived in that huge territory which medieval Icelandic sources call *Svíþióð hin mikla* — "great Sweden" (*Scythia magna*). Archeological research has shown that the Swedes had an important trading-post at Aldeigjuborg from the beginning of the ninth until towards the middle of the eleventh century. A few years ago a little runic inscription came to light on the site of Aldeigjuborg, cut in wood, a find of the greatest cultural and literary interest, and one which may be regarded as clear evidence of the penetration of Swedish culture in the Ladoga area in the ninth century.

From Aldeigjuborg it was no great distance to the important commercial junction called Holmgard (Novgorod). It comes as no surprise to find this great station on the eastern route mentioned in the runic inscriptions of the homeland.

On a boulder at Esta (Södermanland) there is the following inscription, with its suggestion of strife in Holmgard: "Ingefast had this stone cut in memory of Sigvid, his father. He fell in Holmgard, the ship's captain with his crew." The last part of the inscription, as in so many other instances, is in verse:

> *Hann fioll*
> *i Holmgarði,*
> *skæiðaʀ visi,*
> *með skipara.*

Another inscription of interest in this connection is found at Sjusta (Skokloster parish, Uppland).

Plate 10. The Sjusta Boulder, Uppland

Two women, Runa and Sigrid, gave the rune carver Öpir the task of cutting an inscription in memory of four men, Spjallbude, Sven, Andvätt and Ragnar. The four dead men are sons of Runa, a widow; Sigrid is her daughter-in-law, once wife of Spjallbude and now widowed herself. Of him the inscription says: "He died in Holmgard in Olaf's church" — *Hann var dauðr i Holmgarði i Olafs kirkiu.*

When we recall King Olaf Haraldsson's personal connections with Holmgard, it is not particularly surprising that a church dedicated to this martyr-king should have been built there early. This in-

27

scription shows that his sanctity was recognized in Holmgard only a few decades after his death at Stiklestad in 1030. It also throws a revealing light on another aspect of the Viking Age: the death toll in battles clearly assumed devastating proportions.

The way by Ladoga, Aldeigjuborg and Holmgard was the northernmost of the great routes to the east. A more southerly route had still older traditions. Rounding Domesnäs, the northern tip of Kurland, the ships sailed south-east across the Gulf of Riga towards the broad estuary of the Dvina, on whose calm lower reaches the voyage continued eastward through the plains of Semgallen. Here, in Latvia, the existence of large Swedish colonies has been demonstrated by the archeologist.

Both Domesnäs and Semgallen are named on the Mervalla stone (Södermanland), raised by Sigrid in memory of Sven, her husband. The memorial inscription reads thus:

Hann oft siglt	"He often sailed
til Sæimgalla	to Semgallen
dyrum knærri	in dear-prized 'knarr'
um Domisnæs.	round Domesnäs."

Knarr (Old Icelandic *knǫrr*) was the Norseman's name for his roomy sea-going ship, heavier and stronger than the long-ship. The word also occurs in Old English, *cnearr*. (The name possibly arose because the massive hull creaked in the waves — the verb *knarra* is cognate with obsolete English

28

Plate 11. The Mervalla Stone, Södermanland

'gnar(l)' = snarl, growl.) It was the knarr that
carried the Norseman over the great and perilous
oceans to Iceland and Greenland and Vinland the
Good.

The ships were the pride of the Norsemen, their
great technical achievement, and it is natural that
they should often be pictured by the artists of the
time, sung of by the scalds, and named in the inscriptions commemorating the men who sailed them.
It is worth noting that the phrase *dyrum knærri* on
the Mervalla stone has its exact verbal parallel in

a well-known verse by Egill Skalla-Grímsson, composed in 920 according to the chronology of the *Egils saga*. The young poet expresses his yearning for a ship and adventure; he wants to be off with the Vikings —

> *standa upp í stafni,*
> *stýra dýrum knerri*

"stand up in the stem, / steer the dear-prized knarr".

Domesnäs projects into the Gulf of Riga, towards Runö and Ösel, and continues as a reef which gives no safe depth for some miles off the point. It is a treacherous place, hazardous to "dear-prized ships".

Semgallen is Latvian *Zemgale*, which is thought to mean 'the low land'. The Norsemen thus borrowed the name from Latvian. Probably the same thing happened in other cases — evidently, for example, in the name Virland, which in Estonian is *Virumaa*.

This Virland comprises the north-east part of Estonia, lying on the southern shores of the Gulf of Finland. Two men from Uppland fell there, Anund Kåresson and Björn Kättilmundsson. Anund, from the parish of Roslags-Bro in Uppland, *vas drepinn a Virlandi* "was killed in Virland". Björn has two handsome rune stones raised in his memory. One of them, erected in the great grave-field at Lunda, has this inscription: "Ragnfrid had this stone raised in memory of Björn, Kättilmund's son

Plate 12. The Norra Åsarp Stone, Västergötland

and hers. He fell in Virland. God and God's mother help his soul. Åsmund wrote right runes."

Personal names such as Estfare ('Estonia-farer'), Estulv and Est, which appear in runic inscriptions, testify at once to the close connections

Plate 13. The Sjon-
hem Stone, Gotland

with Estonia; originally, Est was probably a slave's
name. Direct evidence of an ill-starred voyage to
Estonia is also preserved on a rune stone in Norra
Åsarp parish in Västergötland: "Guve raised this
stone in memory of Olav, his son, a young man
active and able. He was killed in Estonia. Håvard
carved the stone."

South-west of Domesnäs lies Windau (Latvian
Ventspils, Russian *Vindava*), one of the few harbours

on this flat and unsheltered Baltic coast. It is the nearest harbour for any ship sailing eastward from Gotland. One of the fine Sjonhem stones was probably raised in memory of a man who met his death at the mouth of the river Venta (Windau): *hann varð dauðr a Vindøy.*

Livonia, the country between Semgallen and Estonia, is also mentioned in two inscriptions from central Sweden. From one cut in the rock-face at Åda (Södermanland) we learn that "Härmod had the rock cut in memory of Bergvid, his brother. He was drowned in Livland." And a stone in Uppland preserves the memory of another man who "fell out in Livland".

A runic inscription of another kind deserves notice at this point. It is engraved on a copper box discovered in Sigtuna. In this box was kept a little set of scales for the weighing of gold and silver. Such convenient folding scales were naturally an important part of the merchant's equipment. The owner of the Sigtuna scales had his name inscribed on the box, and he also tells us how they came into his possession. The inscription begins thus: *Diarfʀ fæk af sæmskum manni skalaʀ þessaʀ ... En Værmundr faði runaʀ þessaʀ* — "Djärv obtained these scales from a man from Samland (or Semgallen) ... And Värmund cut these runes." (The rest of the inscription is a curse to frighten thieves away. It consists of two lines in *dróttkvætt*, the noblest of the scaldic metres, and these give the Sigtuna box great value for the history of literature; see p. 123 below.)

Plate 14. The Copper Box from Sigtuna

This inscription is from the beginning of the eleventh century. Sigtuna was then Sweden's most important commercial centre, and it is consequently no surprise that a piece of merchant's equipment like this has come to light there.

The information it gives us about the provenance of Djärv's scales is not altogether precise, since the adjective *sæmskʀ* remains ambiguous for us: *af sæmskum manni* may mean that the man came either from Samland or, possibly, from Semgallen. Samland, famous as the richest source of the highly-prized amber, lies in East Prussia, in the south-east corner of the Baltic.

Before leaving these frequently visited Baltic coast-lands, I should like to speak briefly of one or two inscriptions that tell of men who fell in Finland.

The inscription on a rune stone that once stood in Söderby-Karl parish in Roslagen (Uppland) and is now unfortunately lost said that "Björn and Igulfrid raised the stone in memory of Otrygg, their son. He was killed in Finland" — *a Finnlandi*. This runic inscription, which can be dated to the beginning of the eleventh century, is the oldest Swedish source in which the name of Sweden's eastern neighbour occurs. It is in itself natural that the name should be found on a stone in the coastal district of Roslagen, in the eastern part of Uppland, where many voyages to Finland had — and still have — their beginning. It must however be remembered that the name *Finnland* in Runic Swedish did not have the same significance as it has now. The area to which the name was then applied was certainly only that part which later, typically enough, was to be called Finland Proper, i.e. the south-western part of the country. This coastal area, which is closer to Roslagen than any other part of the Finnish mainland, has thus in time given its name to the whole country. Here we may compare the similar development of the Finnish name for Sweden — *Ruotsi*. Originally this name was probably only used of Roslagen, the coastal district of Uppland, but in time it became the Finnish name for the whole Swedish territory westward over the Baltic. When the rune stone commemorating Otrygg was cut, Swedish had no collective term for the different districts of Finland.

It was in a remoter Finnish province, in Tavast-land, that a man named Egil fell. His stone at Söderby (Gästrikland) tells us: *hann varð dauðr a Tafæistalandi*. He had taken part in a Viking expedition under the chieftain Fröger. Bruse, Egil's brother, had the splendid stone raised to his memory. Åsmund Kåresson and Sven cut the runes. Connections with Tavastland are also attested by the occurrence of the personal name *Tafæistr* in Runic Swedish.

In this connection it may perhaps be recalled that a Swedish military expedition to Finland about the middle of the eleventh century is reported in a source of a completely different kind, *viz.* in Adam of Bremen's *Gesta Hammaburgensis ecclesiæ pontificum*. This important work on the history of the metropolitan see of Hamburg-Bremen was written *c.* 1070—80. Adam says that Anund, son of Emund the Old, "despatched by his father to extend the kingdom, had come to the land of women, whom we think to be Amazons. There he died with all his army from poison which they mixed in their water-springs" (*Et primo quidem filius regis nomine Anund a patre missus ad dilatandum imperium, cum in patriam feminarum pervenisset, quas nos arbitramur Amazonas esse, veneno, quod fontibus immiscuerunt, tam ille quam exercitus eius perierunt*). The "land of women" appears certainly to mean the "land of the Kväner", part of the present Finland, and this amusing misinterpretation must result from a confusion between the two words *kvæn*, 'wife', and the tribal name 'kvän' (*kvæn* is cognate with English 'quean', a common woman, and related to 'queen'). This misunderstanding — 'Quean-land' for 'Kvänland' — has given rise to the legend about Amazons in Finland.

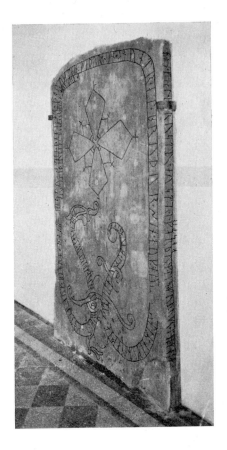

Plate 15.
The Turinge Stone,
Södermanland

We now leave these Baltic coastlands to accompany the Swedes on their travels still further east, following the terse directions of the runic monuments.

Immediately to the east of these coastal regions, as was mentioned above, lay Garðaríki, where large commercial colonies were established along the ancient trade routes. "East in Gardarike" is a familiar expression on the rune stones of central

37

Sweden. It occurs for example in the verse which ends the inscription on the Turinge stone (Söder-manland), the fine poem in which the Södermanland chieftain, Torsten, and his dead brother are commemorated by the surviving members of their family and their retainers:

> *Brøðr vaʀu þæiʀ*
> *bæstra manna*
> *a landi*
> *ok i liði uti.*
> *Heldu sina*
> *huskarla vel.*
> *Hann fioll i orrustu*
> *austr i Garðum,*
> *liðs forungi,*
> *landmanna bæstr.*

"The brothers were / best among men / on land / and out in the levy. / They held their / house-men well. / He fell in action / east in Gardarike, / the levy's captain, / of his land's men the best."

The expeditions to Russia and through Russian territory are thus reflected again and again in the rune stones raised in the home-districts of the voyagers. And memorial runes were also inscribed out on the distant routes themselves.

Near the mouth of the Dnieper, on the island Berezanj in the Black Sea, Grane buried his comrade, Karl. We know this from the rune stone Grane carved and raised there. Karl has his grave on an island whose sheltered bays have given protection

38

to many a Swedish ship on the eastern voyage. When the traveller came from the north, with the perils of the Dnieper cataracts and the difficulties of sand banks and treacherous shoal-water still fresh and stark in his memory, he came at last, here by Berezanj, to open water, where the Black Sea, bigger than the Baltic, opened up before his ship's prow. And when he came to Berezanj from the south — on his way home to the thickly-wooded creeks of Mälaren or the stony havens of Gotland — he could gather strength here before being forced to bend back and oar in the long struggle against the river currents and all the other obstacles on his way. Soon enough the time would come for the unloading and the dragging over the portages and the re-loading, all in the sticky heat of the interior, hardly relieved by the steppe winds and the summer rain. And all the while his longing for a sail-bellying breeze and salt water grew stronger.

Another Swedish inscription which it is natural to mention in company with the Berezanj stone is the one on the Piræus lion. This magnificent marble lion had kept guard in Porto Leone, the harbour of Athens, for many centuries before a Swedish Viking with rune-skilled hand incised his inscription on its flanks. The serpent-band, filled with runes, coils itself round the classic marble in just the same way as on the granite of Uppland. Unfortunately, the inscription is now for the most part illegible, for since it was cut the lion has suffered much from battles in the harbour and from wind and weather.

Plate 16. The Piræus
Lion

The victorious Venetians carried it off as a trophy in
1687 and it now stands in Venice — where its runes
were finally recognized for what they are by a Swedish
diplomat, the Egyptologist Johan David Åkerblad.

The largest and most interesting group of stones
commemorating the eastern expeditions consists,
however, of the so-called Ingvar's stones. They
were raised in memory of men who had followed
Ingvar the Far-travelled on his long journey to
Serkland.

It is impossible to give any fixed boundaries to
the Serkland, 'the Saracens' land', of the rune
stones. The Norsemen probably meant by it the
lands of the Abbasid caliphate, whose capital in the
Viking Age was Bagdad.

Ingvar's expedition is mentioned on nearly thirty rune stones, most of them found in the Mälar region. It undoubtedly attracted many participants and must have been one of the great events in the central Swedish districts in the first half of the eleventh century. The inscriptions show clearly that this bold Viking venture met a dismal end. Not a single one mentions a man who returned from those far-off lands. All the members of the expedition died "south in Serkland".

On a rune stone at Stora Lundby (Söderman-land), for example, we read:

"Spjute and Halvdan, they raised this stone in memory of Skarde, their brother.

> Went east from here
> with Ingvar.
> In Serkland lies
> the son of Öjvind."

Ingvar's expedition has its noblest monument in the inscription on the Gripsholm stone. This stone was set up by Tola in memory of her son, Harald. He was Ingvar the Far-travelled's brother. The inscription ends with this stanza:

Þæiʀ foru drængila	"They fared like men
fiarri at gulli	far after gold
ok austarla	and in the east
ærni gafu.	gave the eagle food.
Dou sunnarla	They died southward
a Særklandi.	in Serkland."

41

Plate 17. The Gripsholm Stone, Södermanland

It should perhaps be mentioned that the phrase "give the eagle food" means to "kill enemies". It is a well-known expression in Eddaic and scaldic verse. Helge Hundingsbane, for example, *sá er opt hefir | ǫrnu sadda* ("who has often sated eagles"), interrupts a flyting between Sinfjötle and Gudmund with the words:

Væri ykkr, Sinfjǫtli,	"More fitting, Sinfjötle,
sæmra miklu	by far for you both
gunni at heyja	to give now battle
ok glaða ǫrnu,	and gladden eagles
en sé ónýtum	than with useless words
orðum at bregðask.	to upbraid each other."

In the poetry of the Vikings, eagle and raven hover over the battle-field, thirsting for the blood of the slain warriors; they sate themselves on the corpses. The wolf, "the horse of the Valkyrie", roams there, hungrily watchful for food (cf. the Rök inscription, p. 14 above). We meet these beasts of battle several times in Old English poetry. In *Beowulf*, the oldest Germanic epic to be preserved entire, all three appear together on the bloodreeking scene. In that part of the great poem where the feuds between the Geats and the Swedes are described, it says, for example: "Music of the harp will not awake the heroes. But the black raven flapping over the dead shall be voluble and tell the eagle of its luck at dinner, when along with the wolf it plundered the slain."

How many ships took part in Ingvar's expedition cannot be determined. Once or twice, it is true, skippers are mentioned who joined him and steered their own ships, but of course we cannot expect the rune stones to give us a complete account of his fleet. On the Svinnegarn stone (Uppland), originally part of an imposing monument that probably stood on the assembly-place at Svinnegarn, parents had the following epitaph inscribed for their son: *Þialfi ok Holmlaug letu ræisa stæina þessa alla at Banka, sun sinn. Es atti æinn seʀ skip ok austr styrði i*

43

Plate 18. The Svinne-
garn Stone, Uppland

Ingvars lið. Guð hialpi and Banka. Æskill ræist. "Tjälve
and Holmlög had all these stones raised for Banke,
their son. He had a ship of his own and steered
eastward in Ingvar's host. God help Banke's soul.
Äskil cut [the runes]."

We hear of another Uppland man in the Steninge
inscription, which is clearly also the work of Äskil,
that "he steered his ship eastward with Ingvar" —
Es styrði austr skipi með Ingvari. The Varpsund stone
is also of interest, raised in memory of the ship's

44

Plate 19. The Varpsund Stone, Uppland

captain Gunnlev, who *vas austr með Ingvari drepinn* (who "was killed in the east with Ingvar"). His memory lives in the brief but pregnant sentence: *Es kunni vel knœrri styra:* "He skilfully could steer a ship".

The fame of Ingvar the Far-travelled spread far and wide. He is the hero of the Icelandic *Yngvars saga víðfǫrla*, where his expedition is described in the romantic style of the so-called legendary sagas (*fornaldarsögur*). The saga, which was written about 300 years after the end of the ill-fated expedition, says there were thirty ships in Ingvar's fleet, but this seems to be something of an exaggeration. The saga must as a whole be characterized as a romantic story woven around a kernel of historical fact. If it were not for the positive and contemporary evidence of the rune stones, then the greatest of all the Swedish Viking enterprises would, like so much else, have been lost to history.

It was not only to win gold and "feed eagles" that men voyaged eastward. Journeys were made to Jerusalem for other reasons.

At Broby bridge in Täby parish, just north of Stockholm, stand two rune stones raised in memory of Östen by his sons and his wife. One of the things that the inscriptions tell us is that Östen "went out to Jerusalem and died in Greece".

Another pilgrimage, also undertaken in the first half of the eleventh century, is attested by the hand-

Plate 20. The Broby Stone, Uppland

some rune inscription which Ingerun, Hård's daughter, had carved as her own memorial at Almarestäket, west of Stockholm. The inscription says that "she wants to go eastward and out to Jerusalem" — *Hon vill austr fara ok ut til Iorsala.*

Langbarðaland, the Norse name for Italy, was

also reached by way of Greece. We are told that Holme, Gudlög's son, who lived in Fittja in Täby parish (Uppland), died *a Langbarðalandi*. And the runic epitaph of Olev from Djulefors (Södermanland) is couched in the following highly-wrought verse, with its ringing alliteration and assonances:

Hann austarla	"He to the eastward
arði barði	ploughed with his prow
ok a Langbarða	and in Langobard's
landi andaðis.	land met his end."

The eastern voyages have also left their traces in the hoards of Arabic coins and oriental jewellery that have been dug up in Swedish soil. These voyages were clearly of great importance from more than one point of view. The commerce with Gardarike, Micklegard and the Orient brought great wealth to the homeland and fostered contacts with the civilisations of Byzantium and the Orient. This eastward movement, which has its literary record in the curt sentences of the rune stones, "takes rank as the most important adventure of the vikings in constructive politics and was certainly the most fateful and significant part played by them in the great drama of European history" (T. D. Kendrick).

ON THE WESTERN ROUTE

We know of a number of men who had made the eastward voyage that they had also "stood like men in the ship's stem" when their course lay in the opposite direction. The Tystberga inscription (Södermanland) says that one of the dead men "had been long in the west", but it also says that he and his father took part in Ingvar's expedition: "They died in the east with Ingvar":

> *Hann hafði vestarla*
> *um veRit længi.*
> *Dou austarla,*
> *með Ingvari.*

These men at the beginning of the eleventh century who, according to the rune stones, had been "westward and eastward", had come into contact with two very different civilisations. There can be no doubt that at first they would feel more at home in the western Germanic world than in the Byzantine-Oriental atmosphere, with its gardens and oases, its desert regions quivering in the heat-haze, its motley multitudes. But in the west too they saw much that was novel and strange. They encountered a highly-developed western culture and made fruitful contact with a politically divided Europe.

The fact that the name England occurs nearly as often as that of Greece in the runic inscriptions of the early eleventh century is enough to show at once that the westward voyages were also common. In several cases, however, the country or countries visited in the west are not defined by name. All that is said of the dead chieftain Spjut, for example, is that "he had been in the west" (Kjula stone, Södermanland):

SaR vestarla
um veRit hafði,
borg um brutna
ok um barða.

"He in the west / had been, / township taken / and attacked."

I said earlier that the eleventh-century westward ventures had to some extent a different character from the voyages to the east. We find however, in one respect at least, a striking external similarity: the Varangian Guard of the Eastern emperors had its parallel institution in the famous body of retainers of Canute the Great, the body-guard called *þingalið* on the rune stones and known as the 'house-carles' in English sources. Membership of this renowned corps of distinguished and well-trained warriors was an honour eagerly sought after. Gere from Kålsta in Häggeby parish (Uppland) was a member, and his sons did not omit mention of it in his memorial inscription: "Stärkar and Hjorvard had this stone raised in memory of their father Gere, who in the west had his place in the *þingalið* (*sum vestr sat i þingaliði*). God help his soul."

A rune stone from Landeryd in Östergötland also deserves mention in this connection. It reads: "Väring raised the stone in memory of Tjälve, his brother, the warrior who served with Canute" (*VæringR ræisti stæin æftiR þialfa, broður sinn, dræng þann, eR vaR meðR Knuti*). It is of some interest to note that the man who raised the stone, the dead man's brother, is

50

Plate 21. The Landeryd Stone, Östergötland

called Väring (= Varangian). In this way the Landeryd stone carries the reader's thoughts both to the Varangians of Micklegard and to the royal body-guard of England.

The name London occurs on the Valleberga stone (Skåne). It was raised in memory of two men, Manne and Svenne, who found their graves in London. The end of the inscription reads: *Guð hialpi sial þæira vel. En þæiʀ liggia i Lundunum* ("May God help their souls well. And they lie in London").

It may be mentioned that two stones with runes on them have been found in the heart of London itself, one of them in St Paul's churchyard. Both

51

(front)　　　　　　　　　　(right side)

Plate 22. The Nävelsjö Stone, Småland

were parts of coffins from the first half of the eleventh
century.

In a similar sort of stone coffin lies Gunnar, Rode's
son, from Småland. He is buried in Bath. His brother
buried him there; his son raised his runic monument

52

at home at Nävelsjö in Småland: "Gunnkel set this stone in memory of Gunnar, his father, Rode's son. Helge laid him, his brother, in a stone coffin in England in Bath" (*Gunnkell satti stæin þenna æftiʀ Gunnar, faður sinn, sun Hroða. Hælgi lagði hann i stæinþro, broður sinn, a Ænglandi i Baðum*).

Stones of especial historical interest are those which mention the Danegeld, i.e. the tribute payments that from the end of the tenth century onwards were imposed on the English people to buy off Viking attacks. (The huge finds of English silver in Swedish soil give some idea of the size of these payments. There are more English silver coins from this period in Swedish museums than there are in England itself.)

To this group belongs the notable Yttergärde stone (Uppland), inscribed between 1020 and 1030. It was raised by Karse and Karlbjörn in memory of their father, Ulv of Borresta, a great yeoman-farmer of Uppland. The inscription reads: "Ulv took in England three gelds. That was the first which Toste paid. Then Torkel paid. Then Canute paid."

This terse statement, with which the sons saw fit to commemorate their dead father, was full of meaning to their contemporaries. An adventurous career is traced here in phrases that could hardly be more laconic. Ulv's contemporaries could not read this inscription without hearing the tempting chink of good English silver. And their ears must have been filled too with the familiar sound and surge of the North Sea waves.

Plate 23. The Ytter-
gärde Stone, Uppland

Toste, who was the first to pay Ulv his share of
the tribute money, was probably the Swedish Viking
chief mentioned once or twice by Snorri Sturluson.
In the *Heimskringla* he writes: "Toste was the name
of a man in Sweden, the mightiest and most re-
spected man in that land of those who had no title
of rank. He was a very great warrior and spent long
periods on campaigns abroad." According to Snorri,
Toste was the father of Sigrid the Ambitious, and
in that case he had as sons-in-law two of the most

renowned figures in this obscure period of Scandinavian history towards the end of the tenth century: the Swedish king, Eric the Victorious, and the Danish king, Sven Forkbeard.

The second leader who distributed payment to Ulv was Torkel the Tall, chief of the Jomsvikings and a figure swathed in legend. He was involved in more than one attack on England in the early years of the eleventh century.

The third was Canute, Sven Forkbeard's son. He became ruler of England at the beginning of 1017, and in 1018 he paid the last and biggest Danegeld to his returning Viking troops. In time he was to show good reason to justify his cognomen 'the Great'. He could justly style himself "Cnuto rex totius Anglie et Denemarcie et Norreganorum et partis Suanorum".

Toste, Torkel and Canute were the names of the leaders in whose wake Ulv of Borresta had sailed to England. They were indeed names that deserved to be recorded on Ulv's rune stone, names that added lustre to the Uppland farmer and his family. And with the rune stone the sons thanked their father for the inheritance he had left them of wealth and honour.

Another Uppland man who "received Canute's payment" and came safely back to his farm was Alle in Väsby. He saw to the preparation of his own monument, on which he records his proud exploit: *Alli let ræisa stæin þenna æftiʀ sik sialfan. Hann tok Knuts giald a Ænglandi. Guð hialpi hans and.* ("Alle

55

Plate 24. The Väsby
Stone, Uppland

had this stone raised to his own memory. He took
Canute's payment in England. God help his soul.")

On one of the Lingsberg stones (Uppland) we
read of Ulvrik that he had taken two payments
in England (*Hann hafði a Ænglandi tu giald takit*).
And on the Grinda stone, also from the first decades
of the eleventh century, it says that Gudve was west
in England and had had his share in the Danegeld
payment — *Guðver var vestr a Ænglandi, gialdi skifti.*

Plate 25. The Lingsberg
Stone, Uppland

Many Swedes at that time might have had the
same memorial as Hävner Torstensson (Bjudby,
Södermanland):

Var til Ænglands
ung$_R$ dræng$_R$ farinn,
varð þa hæima
at harmi dauðr.

"To England had / the young warrior voyaged, /
and later at home / lamented died."

Canute the Great was not the only ruler of England to be named on Swedish rune stones. It is most
likely that it is his son and successor, Harald Hare-
foot, who is referred to on the Tuna stone (Små-

57

Plate 26. The Tuna
Stone, Småland

land): *Tummi ræisti stæin þenna æftiʀ Assur, broður sinn, þann eʀ vaʀ skipari Haralds konungs* ("Tumme raised this stone in memory of Assur, his brother, who was King Harald's seaman").

One of the two Sävsjö stones (Småland) commemorates a man who had held the important post of stallare (marshal) under Håkon Jarl: "Tova raised this stone in memory of Vråe, her father, Håkon

58

Plate 27. The Sävsjö Stone, Småland

Jarl's marshal" —*stallara HakonaR iarls*. We cannot be
perfectly sure who this Håkon Jarl was, but it seems
likely that he was Canute the Great's nephew and
ally, a member of the famous dynasty of the Lade-
jarls of Norway. Håkon was drowned in the Pent-
land Firth in 1029. Tova, daughter of his marshal
from Småland, erects the stone in memory of her

father, proudly conscious of the fact that he had once held one of the highest offices at Håkon Jarl's court. There were, indeed, other voyagers to England in her family; of her father's brother we learn that he "died in England".

A voyage that came to an end before the alluring coasts of England were reached is spoken of on a rune stone from Husby-Lyhundra (Uppland): "Djärv and Orökja and Vige and Joger and Gerhjälm, all these brothers had this stone raised in memory of Sven, their brother. He died in Jutland. He was on his way to England. May God and God's mother help his spirit and soul better than he deserved." The sentence that is of particular interest in this connection reads: *Sar varð dauðr a Iutlandi. Hann skuldi fara til Ænglands.*

Some archeological discoveries made in recent years throw a fascinating light on the contents of this inscription. The sites of two large permanent camps have been uncovered in Jutland, one at Aggersborg on the north side of the Limfjord, and the other at Fyrkat at the head of the Mariagerfjord. These great establishments were evidently military bases, built at the end of the tenth century and in use until nearly the middle of the eleventh. Ships' crews from the whole of Scandinavia foregathered in these camps; here the Vikings had their quarters, received training, and were initiated into the great fraternity of the sea, until at last under strong and resolute captains they sailed out into the North Sea towards the rich goals of France and England.

We know that Viking attacks against England were mounted from the Limfjord. Canute's great invasion fleet collected in its calm sheltered waters in 1015. Like so many others, Sven of the Husby-Lyhundra stone, tempted by reports of the Danegeld, had sailed out to join some foray against England early in the eleventh century. But when the longed-for moment came and the Viking ships were running free with the Jutland coast behind them, Sven was not on board — *saʀ varð dauðr a Iutlandi.* He lies in a Jutish grave, probably at Aggersborg or Fyrkat.

NORTHERN BATTLES

A number of rune stones tell of historical events which were clearly well known at the time they were inscribed, but which we unfortunately can neither locate nor date with certainty. Thus, we do not know for example what battle is meant on the Råda stone (Västergötland): *Þorkell satti stæin þannsi æftiʀ Gunna, sun sinn. Eʀ varð dauðr i orrostu, eʀ barðus kunungaʀ* ("Torkel placed this stone for Gunne, his son. He fell in battle, when the kings fought"). One is naturally tempted to guess that it was the battle of Svöld in the year 1000, when Olaf Tryggvason of Norway fought against Sven Forkbeard of Denmark and Olaf the Swede. But we do not know.

A reference to a sea-battle on one of the rune stones at Fresta church (Uppland), which also undoubtedly dates from the beginning of the eleventh

Plate 28. The Råda Stone, Västergötland

century, is equally obscure: "Gunnar and Sassur, they had this stone raised in memory of Gerbjörn, their father, son of Vitkarl in Svalnäs. Norwegians killed him on Åsbjörn's ship" (*Hann drapu norrmænnr a knærri Asbiarnaʀ*). It may have been in the battle of Svöld that Gerbjörn fell on board the knarr of the sea-captain Åsbjörn, but we must bear in mind that most events of the past have gone unrecorded in history. And when we consider the unusually good opportunities offered in the Viking Age for losing one's life on board ship, we must again admit the impossibility of putting the inscription's statement into any known historical context.

An important battle was evidently fought at Gård-stånga in Skåne. The Forsheda stone (Småland) has this inscription: "Rolf and Äskil raised this stone

Plate 29. The Fresta
Stone, Uppland

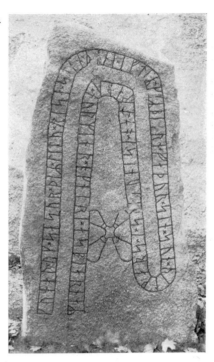

in memory of Livsten, their father. He fell in Skåne
at Gårdstånga. And they carried him home to Finnheden." It has been maintained that this battle took
place during Canute the Great's war against King
Anund Jakob of Sweden and Olaf the Saint of Norway, i.e. during hostilities in Skåne 1025—26. It is
possible, even probable, that Livsten also fell in a
battle "when the kings fought", but we can come no
closer to the historical facts, because Livsten's rune
stone is the only source we have that tells of an
action at Gårdstånga.

63

We are perhaps on firmer ground when we come to identify the historical events that are reflected in the inscriptions on stones at Hällestad and Sjörup (Skåne). They give significant expression to the heroic ideal of loyalty to leader. In considering the relationship between chieftain and retainer, it is illuminating to see here how the dead leader is called brother by his men. On the stone at Hälle-stad we read: *Æskill satti stæin þannsi æftiʀ Toka, Gorms son, seʀ hullan drottin.*

> *Saʀ flo æigi*
> *at Upsalum.*
> *Sattu drængiaʀ*
> *æftiʀ sin broður*
> *stæin a biargi*
> *støðan runum.*
> *Þæiʀ Gorms Toka*
> *gingu næstiʀ.*

"Äskil raised this stone after Toke, Gorm's son, his gracious lord.

> He fled not
> at Uppsala.
> Warriors set up
> after their brother
> the stone on the rock,
> standing firm with runes.
> Toke, Gorm's son,
> they followed nearest."

The same battle at Uppsala is named on the Sjörup stone, where the inscription ends with this homage to the dead man:

> Saʀ flo æigi
> at Upsalum
> en va
> með hann vapn hafði.

"He fled not / at Uppsala / but fought / while he had weapons."

The battle referred to in these inscriptions is very likely that great fight, famous in legend, which took place on the banks of the Fyris river at Uppsala sometime between 980 and 990. It is one of the most celebrated battles in early Scandinavian history, and King Eric of Sweden is supposed to have won his cognomen "the Victorious" because of the defeat he inflicted on his enemies on Fyris fields.

One of the men named on the Högby stone (Östergötland) also appears to have fallen in this battle. Of one of Gulle's five sons it says: "At Fyris fell Åsmund, the unfrightened warrior."

Swedish kings ruled in South Jutland for some decades in the tenth century. Among the evidence which demonstrates the existence of this Swedish dominion are the two rune stones which Astrid, Odinkar's daughter, had raised to the memory of King Sigtrygg, Gnupa's son and hers.

The Swedish kings of South Jutland had their seat in Hedeby — the nodal point for Baltic and North Sea trade and, with Birka in Mälaren, Scandinavia's

Photo: I. Sch

Plate 30. The rune stones of Grinda, Södermanland

66

most important township. From the point of view of commercial policy and power, no place in the North was more rewarding — or more difficult — to rule over. It is not surprising to find this famous name recorded on Swedish rune stones commemorating men who died *i Hæiðaby.*

South of Hedeby, on the other side of the ramparts of the mighty Danevirke, lay the land of the Saxons. The frontier between the Scandinavian North and Saxland was marked by this great defensive wall, which extends right across South Jutland at its narrowest point. One of the Grinda stones in Södermanland commemorates Viking forays against the Saxons; indeed, it mentions both Saxland and England:

Griutgarðr, Æinriði, synir	"Grytgård, Endride, the sons,
giarðu at faður sniallan.	set up after father bold.
Guðver var vestr a Ænglandi,	Gudve was west in England,
gialdi skifti.	geld he divided.
Borgir a Saxlandi	Townships in Saxland
sotti karla.	he attacked like a man."

Finally, the inscription of the Högby stone deserves to be quoted in full; despite one or two uncertainties of interpretation, it offers striking evidence of the restlessness of the Viking Age, of the constant movement on many different routes and

Plate 31. The Högby Stone (back), Östergötland

of the heavy losses in men: "Torgärd raised this stone in memory of Assur, her mother's brother, who died out east in Greece.

> The good farmer Gulle
> had five sons:
> At Fyris fell Åsmund,
> the unfrightened warrior,

Assur died
out east in Greece,
Halvdan was
in holmgang (?) slain,
Kåre *uarþ · atuti.*
Dead is Boe too.

Torkel cut the runes."

(Holmgang, 'island-going', was the technical expression for a formal duel.)

Unfortunately, no certain interpretation of *uarþ · atuti* can be offered. The suggestion that the line should be interpreted as "Kåre died at Dundee" (i.e. at the Scottish port) must be regarded as extremely dubious. But all the same, the Högby stone, inscribed by Torkel at the very beginning of the eleventh century, remains a monument symbolic of all those aspects of Viking Age activity which we have been considering.

Naturally, the Swedish coasts themselves were also liable to attack from foreign fleets. The Bro stone (Uppland) gives us a glimpse of Swedish coastal defence organisation, of the watch that was kept against Vikings: *Ginnlaug, Holmgæiʀs dottiʀ, systiʀ Sygrøðaʀ ok þæiʀa Gauts, hon let gæra bro þessi ok ræisa stæin þenna æftiʀ Assur, bonda sinn, sun Hakonaʀ iarls. Saʀ vaʀ vikinga voʀðr með Gæiti. Guð hialpi hans nu and ok salu.* ("Ginnlög, Holmger's daughter, sister of Sygröd and Göt, she had this bridge made and this stone raised in memory of Assur, her husband, son of Håkon Jarl. He kept watch against the Vikings

69

Plate 32. The Bro Stone, Uppland

with Geter. May God now help his spirit and soul.")
The inscription introduces us to two of the most distinguished among the high-born families of the Mälar
districts, known to us in two other inscriptions from
the beginning of the eleventh century — the Ramsund rock (pp. 139—140 below) and the Kjula stone
(pp. 49—50 above).

Two words of a fragmentary rune stone inscription from Giberga in Södermanland belong to the
same context: ... (þæiʀ) gerðu skipvorð — "... they
kept ship-watch".

A PEACEFUL HOMELAND

It is however not only of warfare, feats of arms and death in distant lands that the Swedish rune stones of the Viking Age can tell us. They can also throw light on peaceful trade and on the labours and aspirations of those who stayed at home.

Trade was a prime mover in the dynamics of the Viking Age. Several of the rune stones described above were without any doubt raised in memory of Swedish merchants who had sailed distant seas. Birka flourished for two hundred years as the centre for transit-trade between East and West. Later, Sigtuna took over the rôle of commercial capital. Here the merchants established their guilds for mutual protection and aid.

Two of Sigtuna's many runic inscriptions well illustrate its commercial connections. One reads: "The guild-brethren of the Frisians had this stone raised in memory of Torkel, their guild-brother. God help his soul. Torbjörn cut [the runes"] (*Frisa gildaʀ letu ræisa stæin þennsa æftiʀ Þorkil, gilda sinn. Guð hialpi and hans. Þorbiorn risti*).

The other inscription is found on a boulder embedded in the ground in the middle of the town; it has a similar message: "The guild-brethren of the Frisians had these runes cut for Albod, Slode's partner. Holy Christ help his soul. Torbjörn cut [the runes]" (*Frisa gi[ldaʀ letu rista runaʀ] þessaʀ æftiʀ Alboð, felaga Sloða. Kristr hinn hælgi hialpi and hans. Þorbiorn risti*).

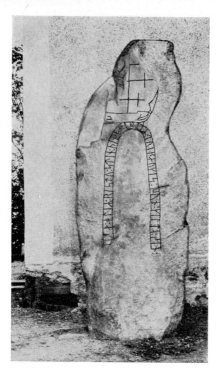

Plate 33. The Törnevalla Stone, Östergötland

To these inscriptions, which give such valuable and interesting insight into the early history of these important social and commercial institutions, the guilds, may be added two more of a similar kind. Both of these rune stones have come to light in Östergötland, and it is significant that the site of each is close to an important centre of commerce and culture. One is situated at Bjälbo, near the ancient trading-centre Skänninge, and the other is at Törnevalla, not far from Linköping.

The Bjälbo stone has this inscription: "Comrades

(*drængiaʀ*) raised this stone in memory of Grep, their guild-brother." The Törnevalla stone, discovered in the autumn of 1960, was raised by members of a guild "after Dräng, Öger's son, their guild-brother" (*æftiʀ Dræng, Øygæiʀs sun, gilda sinn*).

Like the guild of the Frisians in Sigtuna, these guilds of Östergötland must, it seems, have been guilds of merchants. The members of the "Bjälbo guild" and the "Törnevalla guild" were most probably well-to-do yeomen who engaged in trade as well as farming. It seems probable that these Swedish commercial guilds in the last part of the Viking Age were formed on west European models, even though associations of a similar kind had existed earlier within the Norse world.

FARMS AND FARMERS

The farm-names recorded on the rune stones take us also into the home-country. Not a few farmers in the Mälar districts can be — and usually are — proud of the fact that the name of their farm is inscribed on the rune stone they have at home, standing somewhere close to the farmstead or on the slope that long ago was the ancestral burial-ground.

These runic records of place-names are of course the oldest in Sweden, and this lends them special interest. The rune stones show that for the most part the farms had the same names in ancient times as they have now.

73

Plate 34. The Nora Inscription, Uppland

In a number of cases the farm-name was evidently included in the inscription because it was felt important to indicate clearly where the ownership of the land lay. The rune stone then served a double purpose, acting both as a memorial and as a title-deed. It could remind the outside world of how the survivors or descendants had gained possession of their property.

The runic inscription at Nora (Uppland) may be regarded as such a title-deed — one that literally stands as firm as a rock —: *Biorn, Finnviðaʀ sunn, let hoggva hælli þessa æftiʀ Olæif, broður sinn. Hann varð svikvinn a Finnhæiði. Guð hialpi and hans. Eʀ þessi byʀ þæiʀa oðal ok ættærfi, Finnviðaʀ suna a Ælgiastaðum* "Björn, Finnvid's son, had this rock carved in memory of Olev, his brother. He was betrayed [i.e. treacherously killed] on Finnheden. God help his soul. This farm is their *odal* and family inheritance, the sons of Finnvid at Älgesta".

This inscription thus tells of Olev Finnvidsson's violent end on Finnheden (now Finnveden) in southwest Småland. But it is the close of the inscription which attracts our attention at this point.

The place meant by *þessi byʀ* — "this farm" — is Nora, the site of the inscription. The great farm of the sons of Finnvid, Älgesta, lies in Husby-Ärlinghundra parish, nearly twenty miles due north of Nora. The identification of this Älgesta as the family estate of the sons of Finnvid need not be doubted, because we find a rune stone there which says that "Björn, Finnvid's son, had the stone raised to his own memory".

At Ågersta village (Uppland) there is a rune stone, inscribed by Balle, which serves as a boundary mark between two properties. The inscription reads: "Vidhugse had this stone raised in memory of Sä-

Plate 35. The Ågersta Stone, Uppland

rev, his noble father. He lived at Ågersta" (*Hann byggi i Agurstaðum*).

Hiær mun standa	"Here shall stand
stæinn miðli byia.	the stone between farms.
Raði drængʀ	Let that man read
þaʀ rynn se	who rune-wise is
runum þæim	those the runes
sum Balli risti.	that Balle wrote."

A peculiar chain of inheritance is recorded on the rune-inscribed rock at Hillersjö (Uppland), where the passer-by is also exhorted to "interpret the runes"

Plate 36. The rune-inscribed rock at Hillersjö, Uppland

— *raða runum:* "Interpret the runes! Germund took Gerlög to wife when she was a maid. Later they had a son, before Germund was drowned. Afterwards the son died. Then she had Gudrik as her husband. He . . .[1] Then they had children. Of them only a girl lived; she was called Inga. Ragnfast of Snottsta took her to wife. Afterwards he died and then the son. And the mother took the inheritance after her son. Inga afterwards had Erik as her husband. Then she died. Then Gerlög came into the inheritance after Inga, her daughter. Torbjörn Scald cut the runes."

[1] Part of the inscription is destroyed here, with the loss of about 25 runes.

The Viking Age rules of inheritance that were applied in this case agree with the statutes of the Uppland law, codified in 1296.

Ragnfast of Snottsta (*i · snutastaþum*) is known from four other inscriptions at home on his patrimonial estate; they were made in his memory by Inga, his wife, also mentioned on the Hillersjö inscription above. In one of the inscriptions we read: "Inga had the runes cut for Ragnfast, her husband. He alone owned this farm after Sigfast, his father. God help their souls." In another of these Snottsta inscriptions we find a direct connection with the one at Hillersjö: "Inga raised staff and stones in memory of Ragnfast, her husband. She came into the inheritance after her child."

The history of another inheritance is traced in the inscriptions on the two Hansta stones (Spånga parish, Uppland). The stones were raised in memory of the brothers, Ärnmund and Ingemund, who had died in Greece. The inscriptions read: *Gærðarr ok Iorundr lata ræisa þessa stæina æftiʀ systursyni sina Ærnmund ok Ingimund. Þessun mærki æru gar æftiʀ syni Inguʀ. Hon kam þæiʀa at arfi, en þæiʀ brøðr kamu hænnaʀ at arfi, Gærðarr brøðr. Þæiʀ dou i Grikkium* ("Gärdar and Jorund had these stones raised in memory of their sister's sons, Ärnmund and Ingemund. — These signs are made in memory of Inga's sons. She came into the inheritance after them [i. e. Ärnmund and Ingemund], and the brothers — Gärdar and his brother — came into the inheritance after her. They [i.e. Ärnmund and Ingemund] died in Greece").

The sequence of inheritance had thus gone in this way: Ärnmund and Ingemund had succeeded to their patrimonial estate on their father's death. They had then made the traditional journey to Greece, where they lost their lives. The inheritance of the dead brothers had then passed to Inga, their mother, and on her death it went to her brothers, Gärdar and Jorund. These, in gratitude, then raised the two rune stones to the memory of their nephews, dead in Greece.

We learn the names of some members of Swedish Viking Age families from these inscriptions at Hillersjö, Snottsta and Hansta. Sometimes we come to know a family through several generations.

This is particularly the case with the Malsta stone in Rogsta parish (Hälsingland). In this inscription we can trace an ancient family through seven generations. It must undoubtedly also have had a legal purpose. It is a significant fact, and one of no small interest to any student of Sweden's ancient culture, that this inscription is written in the so-called Hälsinge runes. These runes might be called the shorthand of the ancients — they were developed for practical use, for records of various kinds, and only in rare and exceptional cases were they used for memorial inscriptions on the rune stones. In these it was natural that people should prefer the monumental forms of the runic letters, more appropriate to their ceremonial purpose.

The Malsta stone bears this inscription: "Frömund raised this stone in memory of Rike-Gylve, Bräse's son. And Bräse was Line's son, and Line was Ön's son, and Ön was Ofeg's son, and Ofeg was Tore's son. Groa was Rike-Gylve's mother, and she then bore Ladvi and later Gudrun. Frömund, Rike-Gylve's son, cut these runes. We fetched this block of stone from the headland at Balsten. Gylve acquired this district and also three estates further north; he also acquired Lönnåker and afterwards Färsjö."

Another remarkable stone from this point of view is at Sandsjö (Småland), where six generations are counted: "Arnvard had this stone raised after Hägge, his father, and after Hära, his father, and Karl, his father, and Hära, his father, and Tegn, his father, and after these five forefathers."

It is the Norseman's inborn interest in genealogy, clearly much alive in ancient times, that we meet in these last inscriptions.

Just one more farm-name occurring in a Viking Age inscription will be discussed at this point. At Lövhamra in Skepptuna parish (Uppland) there is a rune stone raised in memory of *ulf* × *i lukobri*, which must undoubtedly be read as 'Ulf i Laugham-bri'. The rune stone's farm-name thus differs from the present Lövhamra. On the other hand, there can be no doubt whatever that the original form of the name is the one appearing on the rune stone. The first element is the word *laug*, 'bath', found for example in the Scandinavian word for Saturday, *lördag* (*laugardagr*), properly 'bath-day'. Later, when both the bathing-place there and the word *laug* had gone out of use, the farm-name was given a new

Plate 37. The Lövhamra Stone, Uppland

form, the inappropriate Lövhamra (*löv-* is English *leaf-*).

Names of Swedish provinces and larger districts also appear sometimes on the rune stones. We have already met examples of both kinds (*Skanøy*, Skåne, *Finnhæiðr*, Finnveden, see pp. 63, 75 above). An important district in Södermanland is named on the Aspa stone, found in 1937 near the old assembly-place of Rönö hundred. Two Södermanland magnates have their epitaphs on the stone: *Astrið let gæra kumbl þausi at Anund ok Ragnvald, sun sinn.*

> *Urðu dauðiʀ i Danmarku*
> *vaʀu rikiʀ a Rauningi*
> *ok sniallastiʀ i Sveþiuðu.*

81

Plate 38. The Aspa Stone, Södermanland

"Astrid had this memorial raised after Anund and Ragnvald, her son.

> They died in Denmark —
> were men of rank in Röninge —
> and swiftest of deed in Sweden."

The Astrid who raised this imposing rune stone was thus wife of Anund and Ragnvald was their son. It is possible moreover that another rune stone introduces us to more members of the same family. Some ten years ago a rune stone with the following inscription came to light at Lunda, a good twenty miles from Aspa: "Halvdan raised this stone after Ragnvald, his father, and after Dan, his brother, able men." Now, the fact is that the name Ragnvald was still very rare in the eleventh century. The only examples known from the whole of Södermanland are precisely these two occurring on relatively recently discovered stones. In the Viking Age it was a nobleman's name, reserved for members of the greatest families, a fact which accounts for its rarity. It is consequently possible that we meet members of the same family both at Aspa and Lunda, although, as must often be the case, we cannot be positive about the identification. Confirmation could only be gained by the discovery of yet another rune stone from the same milieu.

Another venerable district-name stands on a rune stone which I was fortunate enough to discover in the autumn of 1959. We read here: "Honäv raised the stone after Germar, his father. He died in Tjust. Skamhals hewed these runes."

This is a valuable record, the oldest we now have, of the name of Tjust, the coastal district in Småland. The name of the people of Tjust — the tribal name, that is — appears in a much older source, the *De origine actibus que Getarum*, by the Gothic

Plate 39. The Västerljung Stone, Södermanland

historian Jordanes (sixth century). In a list of Swedish tribes or "nationes" he includes *theu(s)tes*, which can hardly mean anything but the people of Tjust.

If we may judge by the information imparted by the rune stones, there were three kinds of peaceful public works undertaken in the home-districts that were considered of special importance: clearing roads, building bridges, and establishing assembly- or Thing-places (on these last see pp. 103—12).

Bridge-building is mentioned particularly often, carried out to commemorate dead kinsfolk in this world and to ease their passage into the next. This custom was undoubtedly connected with the activity of the missionary church in Sweden. Roads that were serviceable in all weathers were essential if people were to come to God's house. To build bridges and to clear tracks over difficult terrain thus became pious acts, which men believed to be an efficacious means of helping the soul through the searching fires of purgatory. In this way the eleventh century in Sweden was a road-building epoch.

The word bridge in the runic inscriptions usually meant a causeway over marshland or a stone-laid ford over water-courses that crossed important roads.

There are still many places in Sweden today where the main road crosses the "bridge" that was first built in the Viking Age. An inscription in Södertälje, on a cliff-face just by the road, reads: "Holmfast had the way cleared (*let braut ryðia*) and the bridge made in memory of Gammal, his father, who lived in Näsby. God help his soul. Östen cut [the runes]."

85

Plate 40. The Södertälje Inscriptions, Södermanland

The most famous of all these rune-stone bridges is Jarlabanke's bridge at Täby (Uppland). Jarlabanke put up four rune stones by the bridge, two facing each other at the north end and two at the south end. The bridge was also flanked by smaller standing-stones (so-called *bautasteinar*), without runes on them. The length of the bridge was about 380 feet, its width 21 feet.

All four rune stones have practically identical inscriptions: "Jarlabanke had these stones raised in memory of himself while he still lived. And he built this bridge for his soul. And alone he owned the whole of Täby. God help his soul." There can be no doubt that his causeway was once one of Sweden's

Plate 41. One of the rune stones at Jarlabanke's Bridge

most impressive rune-stone bridges. (On another imposing roadway see pp. 111—12 below.)

A rune stone at Åby in Lena parish (Uppland), originally erected as a road sign on the banks of the river Fyris, has this inscription: "Nase and his brothers raised this stone in memory of Jarl, their

Plate 42. The Sälna Stone, Uppland

noble father. And they made the bridge to please God."

There is another among the many "bridge inscriptions" of Uppland that deserves notice. It is cut on the natural rock-face at Näs in Frösunda parish, and here again the motive of Christian piety is clearly in evidence: "Livsten had the bridges made for his soul's health and for that of Ingerun, his wife, and of his sons, Jorund and Niklas and Luden."

A splendid bridge-monument is the Sälna stone (Uppland). We can feel the bridge-builders' pride in their work as we read: *Øystæinn ok Iorundr ok Biorn þæiʀ brøðr ræispu . . . , faður sinn. Guð hialpi hans and ok selu, forgefi hanum sakaʀ ok syndiʀ.*

> *Æi mun liggia*
> *með aldr lifiʀ*
> *bro harðslagin,*
> *bræið æft goðan.*
> *Svæinaʀ gærðu*
> *at sinn faður.*
> *Ma æigi brautaʀ kuml*
> *bætra verða.*

"Östen and Jorund and Björn, those brothers raised [this stone after . . .], their father. May God help his spirit and soul, forgive him offences and sins. Always will lie / while ages live / the bridge firmfounded / broad after the good man. / The boys made it / in memory of their father. / No bridgemonument / can be better made."

On a boulder at Runby, situated in an important

Plate 43. One of the inscriptions on the Runby Boulder, Uppland

position on the network of waterways in Uppland, are two inscriptions, which read as follows: "Ingrid had the *laðbro* made and the stone cut after Ingemar, her husband, and after Dan and after Banke, her sons. They lived in Runby and owned the farm there. Christ help their souls.

This shall stand in memory of the men
as long as menfolk live."

The *laðbro* was probably a quay or jetty for loading vessels, an amenity which must have been of the greatest importance to the inhabitants of this central district.

As said above, the modern main roads of Sweden are in many places bordered by rune stones that tell us who first built the way on which we now travel. But some stones are also located in places where traces of an ancient path are now only to be found with difficulty, amongst rocks and brushwood. In this way the location of rune stones can sometimes give us useful information about the land routes of the Viking Age, once important but now otherwise lost.

Another work of general public benefit, also intended to make communications easier, was the building of *sæluhus*, hospices or shelters. Such huts for the use of weary and weather-beaten travellers have been found in several districts, where the roads lie far from the settlements.

A rune stone, unfortunately damaged, at Karberga in Funbo parish (Uppland) bears witness to this custom: "Ingrid and Ingegärd had the stone raised and the ford made in the channel in memory of Tore, their father. Tore had the hospice built in memory of Ingetora, his wife, and in memory of . . ."

On an Uppland rune stone at Gryta in Kulla parish and on a stone in Aspö church in Södermanland, it says that the surviving members of the family have had built *likhus : auk : bru* — lik-house and bridge. The combination of the two words makes it tempting to identify the first element in *likhus* as *likn*, 'mercy' — although the compound *liknhus* is not found elsewhere — and to regard it as meaning 'house of mercy', another form of *sæluhus* or hospice. It is possible however to offer another interpretation.

The word *likhus* may mean literally 'corpse-house' (cf. *lik* with the first element in English lyke-wake, lich-gate), and it may have denoted a monument in the form of a little house built over a grave. Such 'grave-houses' have an ancient Christian tradition behind them, but it will be enough here to mention only their appearance in the early Germanic world. A statute in the laws of the Salic Franks says: "If anyone damages the house in the form of a basilica which has been set up over a dead man, let him pay thirty solidi in atonement." One would presume that Viking Age 'corpse-houses' in Sweden were made of wood, which perished as time passed on. We know, in fact, that the custom of erecting little houses over graves survived for hundreds of years in Sweden, and such buildings, the so-called *gravrord* (*-rol*, *-ror*), were still common in the eighteenth century. If this interpretation of *likhus* is correct, we learn something of the burial customs of the Viking Age. We should find here constructions in wood corresponding to the so-called Eskilstuna sarcophagi and other grave monuments in stone. I shall return to these later.

THE CONVERSION

In connection with these laudable acts, bearing witness as they do to a Christian public spirit, it is appropriate to cite a few inscriptions whose mode of expression is characteristic of the Christian missionary age in Sweden.

The interesting phrase "to die in white clothes"

92

Plate 44. Figures on a rune stone from Kalmar Church, Uppland

occurs on several Uppland rune stones. The Amnö stone says: "Ingelev had this stone raised after Brune, her husband. He died in Denmark in white clothes. Balle cut [the runes]" (*Hann varð dauðr a Danmarku i hvitavaðum*). The Torsätra stone reads: *Unna let ræisa þennsa stæin æftiʀ sun sinn Øystæin, sum do i hvitavaðum. Guð hialpi salu hans* ("Unna had this stone raised after her son, Östen, who died in white clothes. God help his soul"). The Molnby stone says: "Holmlög and Holmfrid had the stones raised after Faste and Sigfast, their sons. They died in white clothes" (*þæiʀ dou i hvitavaðum*). The Håga stone in Bondkyrka parish was put up by parents in memory of their son. He died *i hvitavaðum i Danmarku.*

The *hvitavaðiʀ*, 'white clothes', baptismal robes, were worn by the convert at his baptism and for the week following. The Upplanders in whose memory this group of rune stones was raised were thus baptised on their deathbed. It is the missionary period, the age of conversion, that we encounter in these inscriptions — their language is the language of the Norse church, and those who set up the stones found consolation in the knowledge that their close kinsmen had avoided eternal punishment by accepting baptism as their last hour drew near.

It is typical that two of the dead men named in these inscriptions are said to have been baptised in Denmark. Voyages by Swedish men to countries where the new faith had long been established — England, Greece, Denmark, Saxland and others — were naturally of great significance for the introduction of Christianity in Sweden itself.

The language of the missionary period is already to be found on rune stones from the beginning of the eleventh century. The prayer formula which the sons of Ulv of Skålhamra had inscribed on his monument is extremely illuminating (Risbyle, Täby parish): *Ulfkætill ok Gyi ok Unni þæiʀ letu ræisa stæin þenna æftiʀ Ulf, faður sinn goðan. Hann byggi i Skulhambri. Guð hialpi hans and ok salu ok Guðs moðiʀ, le hanum lius ok paradis* ("God and God's mother help his spirit and soul, grant him light and paradise").

This prayer for the gift of heavenly light and

94

Plate 45. The Risbyle Stone, Uppland

paradise to the soul of the dead man is found on two other stones, one from Uppland and one from Bornholm.

The Uppland stone stands at Folsberga in Vallby parish; its inscription ends with the prayer: *Kristr lati koma and Tumma i lius ok paradisi ok i þann hæim bæzta kristnum* ("May Christ let Tumme's soul come into light and paradise and into the world best for Christians").

On the Bornholm stone (Klemensker 1) the formula is found twice: "Gunnhild had this stone raised after Ödbjörn, her husband. May Christ help Ödbjörn's soul to light and paradise. — Christ and Saint Michael help the souls of Ödbjörn and Gunnhild to light and paradise." It may be mentioned in passing that the archangel Michael is also invoked on an Uppland rune stone at Ängby, Knivsta parish, where the inscription ends thus: *Mihel gætti and hans* ("Michael take care of his soul").

The inscriptions that have just been quoted indicate that the missionary church in Scandinavia expressed itself in a uniform language. The task of the missionary in Sweden — obviously an arduous one — is here in a nutshell: Valhall is exchanged for the word *paradis*, Thor and mysterious magic charms are replaced by God and God's mother, Christ and Saint Michael.

The heavenly light is also found in an inscription at Kimstad (Östergötland): "Sven and his brothers raised the stone in memory of their father, Jarl. God and God's mother help his soul *i lius*" ('into light').

Another prayer formula, one which also shows a truly Christian frame of mind, is found on a number of rune stones, most of them set up in the first decades of the eleventh century. The Eggeby stone in Spånga (Uppland) may serve as an example: *RagnælfR let gærva bro þessi æftiR Anund, sun sinn*

*goðan. Guð hialpi hans and ok salu bætr þæn
hann gærði til.*

> *Munu æigi mærki
> mæiʀi verða,*

moðiʀ gærði æftiʀ sun sinn æiniga.

"Ragnälv had this bridge made in memory of Anund,
her good son. May God help his spirit and soul
better than he deserved (literally, 'better than
he did towards it'). No monuments shall be better.
The mother made it for her only son." Slight
variations on the same theme occur elsewhere: *Guð
biargi sel hans bætr þæn hann hafʀ til gært* "God save
his soul better than he deserved" (Brössike, Södermanland). On the Lilla Lundby stone it has this
form: *Guð hialpi sal hans bætr þæn hann kunni til gærva*
("God help his soul better than he knew how to
deserve it").

In these petitions we must naturally see the humble
hope that God will let mercy temper justice when
the time comes to pronounce doom over a poor and
sinful creature. Such expressions must of course not
be taken — as they recently have been — to mean
that the dead man was a heathen or a particularly
bad Christian. It is Christian humility which here
speaks in the rune stone's voice. The formula has
the same significance as the Sälna stone's petition
for forgiveness of the dead man's "offences and sins"
(see p. 89 above).

The end of the inscription on a stone found a few
years ago in Uppsala deserves to be quoted in

97

Plate 46. The Källbyås Stone, Västergötland

this connection: *Guð signi oss, gumna valdr, hæilagʀ drottinn* ("May God bless us, ruler of men, holy lord").

Of the people who raised these last-named monuments we might use the words that stand as Fare's memorial on the Källbyås stone (Västergötland): *Saʀ hafði goða tro til Guðs* ("He had good faith in God").

The rune stones show in a variety of ways what important changes Christianity brought about in the social life of the Viking Age. Undoubtedly, one of the most radical changes was that the dead man was now to be buried in the consecrated ground of the churchyard, separated from his kin. He was no longer to lie in his grave on the slopes by the homestead where his ancestors lay. An archaic provision in the church section of the Uppland law-code leaves a deep impression of the cleavage this meant between old custom and new faith: "No one shall sacrifice to idols and no one shall put faith in groves or stones. All shall honour the church, thither all shall go, the quick and the dead, those who come into the world and those who go from it." (... *Allir skulu kirkiu dyrkæ, þit skulu allir, baþi quikkir ok døþir, komændi ok farændi i weruld ok aff.*)

Venerable custom and family tradition were broken, and the new obligations were enunciated in the ecclesiastical sections of the provincial laws. As a point of interest, it may be noted that the earliest legal provision of an ecclesiastical nature preserved in Old Swedish is found incised in runes on a ring of forged iron that now belongs to Forsa church in Hälsingland. In all probability there was much use made of runic writing for the recording of such legal statutes.

The new burial customs have found expression on one or two rune stones. The Bogesund stone gives us one testimony: "Gunne and Åsa had this stone raised and (made this) coffin of stone in memory of ... their son. He died at Ekerö. He is buried in the churchyard. Fastulv cut the runes. Gunne raised this slab of rock." It is interesting to observe that in this transition period a rune stone was evidently raised in the ancestral cemetery at home, while a more ecclesiastical sort of monument was provided in the churchyard at Ekerö.

A rune stone stands at Bjärby bridge, Runsten parish (Öland), raised in memory of Fastulv by his wife and sons. From it we learn that *hann eR grafinn i kirkiu*. This must, it seems, mean that he had his grave inside the church itself, a very honourable place, both then and now. Burial in consecrated ground is probably also indicated by the inscription on a rune stone, unfortunately damaged, from the ruin of St Pers (Peter's) church in Sigtuna. It ends by saying that the stone was erected by a man, *sem hana førði til Sigtunum* (sic). The dead person, a woman, seems thus to have been brought for burial to Sigtuna, at this time the stronghold of the missionary church in Uppland.

The rune stones can thus tell us of the building of churches in Sweden at the end of the Viking

Plate 47. The Frösö Stone. A drawing from the 17th century

Age, although of course we also have other sources of information about their existence.

It should be observed in this connection that the change in burial customs may not always have been so deeply felt after all. The fact is that in a surprising number of cases the site chosen for the new enclosed churchyard adjoins some ancient family burial ground with all its traditional associations. In such cases, perhaps, the break in custom did not seem so definitive, at any rate for the family on whose land the church was built.

The conversion of a whole province towards the middle of the eleventh century finds unambiguous record in the inscription on the stone that stands in Frösön (Jämtland): "Östman, Gudfast's son, had this stone raised and this bridge made, and he had Jämtland christianised. Åsbjörn made the bridge. Tryn and Sten cut these runes."

It seems likely that the conversion of Jämtland was the result of a decision taken at the assembly of the Jämtlanders, where Östman perhaps held office as law-man. In that case, we should have here a parallel, on a modest scale, to the momentous decision of the Icelandic Althing, when this national assembly adopted Christianity in the year 1000, a few decades before the conversion of Jämtland. Denmark had become Christian some years earlier, about A.D. 985, as is shown by the famous Jelling stone: "King Harald commanded these *kuml* (monuments) to be made after Gorm, his father, and after Tyre, his mother, that Harald who won all Denmark and Norway and made the Danes Christian."

The information preserved on the rune stones thus enables us to draw some conclusions concerning the advance of Christianity in Sweden. Grave monuments with runic inscriptions also give us valuable information about the period that followed the missionary age itself. (See pp. 155—60 below.)

I have mentioned (p. 85) certain works, under-taken to give glory to God and eternal joy to the souls of the dead. A work of general public benefit and one that also met a social need was the laying-out of a Thing-place, where the local court met.

Modern building has fortunately not yet disturbed the Thing-place at Bällsta in Vallentuna parish (Upp-land). Two rune stones stand there, with an inscrip-tion that begins on the one and continues on the other: "Ulvkel and Arnkel and Gye, they made here a Thing-place.

> There shall no mightier
> memorial be found
> than the one Ulv's sons
> set up after him,
> active lads
> after their father.
> They raised the stones
> and made the staff,
> the splendid one
> as a sign of honour.
> Likewise Gyrid
> loved her husband.
> So a song of sorrow
> sustains his memory.

Gunnar hewed the stone."

What interests us at this point is that the sons laid out an assembly-place on this beautiful site, by the shore of the Vallentunasjö, where the rune stones

stand. As far as one can see, however, the Thing-place
remained in use for only a few decades — a surprising conclusion but plausible if we are to
accept the evidence of another rune stone in the
same parish — the Jarlabanke stone at Vallentuna
church. The inscription here is cut on both sides of
the stone and reads: *Iarlabanki let ræisa stæin þenna
at sik kvikvan. Hann atti æinn Tæby allan. Guð hialpi
and hans. | Iarlabanki let ræisa stæin þenna at sik kvikvan,
ok þingstað þenna gærði, ok æinn atti alt hundari þetta.*

One of the interesting facts that we learn from
this inscription is that, while he lived, Jarlabanke
"made this Thing-place, and alone owned the whole

Plate 48 b. The Bällsta Stone 2, Uppland

of this hundred". The phrase suggests that this assembly-place was intended to serve the whole of the Vallentuna hundred. According to the provincial laws, there was to be one Thing-place in each "hundred". In passing, it may be noted that Jarlabanke's statement that he owned the whole hundred contains a serious — but significant — exaggeration. In fact, he was probably the king's *bryti* or steward in charge of the Vallentuna district, and possibly it was because of this that he called himself Jarlabanke. At any rate, it seems a reasonable assumption that he was the leader of the assembly, its law-man.

Jarlabanke's establishment of a new Thing-place, quite near the one laid out only twenty or thirty

105

Plate 49. The Jarlabanke Stone (back) at Vallentuna Church, Uppland

years earlier at Bällsta, might be explained in the following way. Jarlabanke has now become the most powerful man in the district. It would hardly be possible for him to preserve his equanimity as he entered the Thing-place at Bällsta, where the rune stones and "splendid staff" (*stafʀ hinn mikli*) would constantly remind him, and everyone else at the assembly, of the family of Ulv of Skålhamra, until recently the greatest and most influential landowners in the locality. We know this Skålhamra family from the clear evidence of a number of rune stones. There is good reason to suppose that Jarlabanke was all too jealous of his own honour to be able to tolerate, before his very eyes at the assembly-place, the sight of the proud verses which the sons of Ulv had inscribed in their father's honour. No one was more anxious than Jarlabanke to take care of his own obituary by means of rune-inscribed monuments; no one has taken such pains as he to preserve the memory of his own greatness.

A great pillar or "staff" had been raised on the Thing-place at Bällsta in memory of Ulv. This custom is also attested in some other inscriptions. On the Vreta stone (Uppland) it says that "Inga raised staff and stones after Ragnfast, her husband", and from the rune stone at Kolsundet (Södermanland) we learn that "Ingefrid had the stone and staff raised after Öulv, her father". It is probably the same custom that is implied in the Fyrby inscription, which is all in verse:

> Iak væit Hastæin
> þa Holmstæin brøðr
> mænnr rynasta
> a Miðgarði.
> Sættu stæin
> ok stafa marga
> æftiʀ Frøystæin
> faður sinn.

Plate 50. The Fyrby Inscription, Södermanland

"I know Håsten / and Holmsten, brothers, / to be men rune-wisest / in Middle-gard [i.e. the world]. / They set up the stone / and many 'staves' / after Frösten, / the father of them."

On a rune stone that once did service in the doorway of the now ruined church of Stora Ryttern (Västmanland) occur the words: "Gudlev set up staff and these stones after Slagve, his son ..."

This custom is described and light thrown on it from an unexpected quarter — in a source that is completely different in kind and about a century older than these rune stones. During his travels in Russia in 921–2 the Arabian diplomat, Ibn Fadlan, had the opportunity of witnessing at first hand the funeral of a Norse chieftain. When Ibn Fadlan arrived, the chieftain's ship had already been dragged ashore and preparations for the funeral ceremonies begun. The end of his extraordinarily interesting description deserves to be quoted in full: The nearest kinsman first kindled the funeral pyre and then everyone helped to make it burn. In less than an hour the ship, the timber, the girl and the dead man had been reduced to ashes. Then on the place where the ship, dragged up out of the water, had stood, something like a circular mound of earth was thrown up. In the middle of the mound they erected a thick pillar of birch wood, and on it they cut the dead man's name and the name of the king of the Rus. Then they went on their way. — There seems little doubt but that the birch wood pillar in Ibn Fadlan's account corresponds to the 'staff' mentioned on the rune stones. The inscriptions' alliterative phrase, 'staff and stones', evidently refers to a custom with a long tradition behind it.

An assembly-place must, of course, have been a distinguished site for a rune stone. It had a central

Plate 51. The Stora Ryttern Stone, Västmanland

position in the district and all the members of the assembly had its inscription before their eyes. On the Thing-place at Aspa (Södermanland) stands the rune stone which Tora raised in memory of her husband, Öpir, who had fought *vestarla*, 'in the west':

Stæinn saʀsi	"This stone
standr at Øpi	stands after Öpir,
a þingstaði	on the Thing-place,
at Þoru ver.	after Thora's man."

The finest rune stone in Västmanland stands on the Thing-place at Badelunda. We may take it for

Plate 52. The rune stone at Badelunda, Västmanland

granted that the men whose names are recorded on it belonged to the greatest family in the district at the beginning of the eleventh century. The inscription reads: "Folkvid had all these stones raised after Heden, his son, Anund's brother. Vred cut the runes."

Since it is beyond all doubt that the rune stone has always stood in the same place, the phrase "all these stones" must refer to stones which are, or were, to be found in the immediate vicinity of Heden's monument. A few years ago I made a preliminary survey of the site and was then able to show that at any rate some of these stones were still there — sunk deep in the ground and hidden for centuries. In the autumn of 1960 excavation of the area around the rune stone was begun by members of the staff of the State Department of Antiquities, and the work was completed in the spring of 1961. We found fourteen of the original standing-stones (*bautasteinar*), lying in a long, straight row.

It is clear that Heden's memorial had consisted of a roadway constructed on a truly grand scale: an avenue, flanked by a long row of standing-stones, which had led from the river-ford on the northeast to the Badelunda ridge on the southwest. At the centre of this stretch of roadway stood the rune stone. It is of particular interest that "all these stones" border Eriksgata; see p. 23 above. The complete lay-out of the memorial that has now been discovered has been damaged by the removal of two of the standing-stones in connection with cultivation of the land around the rune stone. All the same, we can see what the original scale of the roadway was like, and it may be justly called Sweden's proudest 'bridge'-monument from the Viking Age. (On bridge-building see p. 85 f.)

THE GOOD MAN

A man's distinction as sailor, warrior or public benefactor was not the only subject of eulogy in the runic inscriptions. Qualities such as generosity, benevolence and eloquence also find record in the memorials inscribed to the dead.

The epitaph of the dead brothers on the Turinge stone (see p. 38 above) includes the statement: "they maintained their house-men well". Generosity was a characteristic of the chieftain, often praised in the ancient poetry. The little runic stanza on the Turinge stone expresses the same thoughts as are found, for example, in *Beowulf*, when in the last scene of the epic the retainers stand lamenting round the burial mound of the hero:

Swa begnornodon	"So they mourned,
Geata leode	the men of the Geats,
hlafordes hryre,	their captain's loss,
heorðgeneatas;	his hearth-companions;
cwædon þæt he wære	they said him to be
wyruldcyninga	of all the world's sovereigns
manna mildust	the most munificent
ond monðwærust,	and the most gentle,
leodum liðost	kindest to his people
ond lofgeornost.	and keenest for fame."

An Uppland rune stone (Västra Väppeby, Veckholm parish) praises the dead man as "a man generous with food and eloquent" — *mandr mataʀ goðr ok malsrisinn*. On another stone (Gådö, Boglösa parish) Holmbjörn sings his own praises as a man "liberal with food and eloquent" — *mildr mataʀ ok malsrisinn*.

A rune stone at Krageholm, Sövestad parish, in Skåne, ends its inscription with these words of praise: *hann vaʀ bæztr bomanna ok mildastr mataʀ* ("he was the best of yeomen and the most liberal with food").

Plate 53. The Västra
Väppeby Stone, Upp-
land

The same qualities are given prominence in a stanza
on the Ivla stone (Småland). The stone was raised
by Vimund in memory of his brother, Sven:

> *mildan við sinna*
> *ok mata*R *góðan,*
> *i orðlofi*
> *allra miklu*

"gentle with his folk / and generous with food, / in
great esteem / with all people".

The ancient poem *Hávamál* provides close parallels
to the expressions found on the rune stones:

> *Fannka ek mildan mann*
> *eða svá matar góðan*

"I did not find so free a man / nor one with food so liberal".

The noun *oniðingR* (literally, 'un-dastard') is used in a number of verse-inscriptions to denote an outstanding and generous man. The Transjö stone (Småland) says this of the dead man:

> *Hann vaR manna*
> *mestr oniðingR.*
> *ER a Ænglandi*
> *aldri tynði.*

"He was among men / the most 'un-dastard'. / He in England / lost his life." That generosity was a highly prized personal quality is suggested too by the name *Osnikinn* which appears in some inscriptions; it originally meant 'the un-greedy'.

In the busy times of sowing and harvest a farmer might well find himself abroad in Russia, Greece, Saxland or England, or held up in a ship on the North Sea or the Black Sea. The responsibility of running the farm in his absence rested then on the shoulders of his wife. A Swedish housewife receives well-deserved homage on the Fläckebo stone (Västmanland), set up by Holmgöt of Hassmyra in memory of Odindisa, his wife: "There will not come to Hassmyra a better mistress, who looks after the farm. Balle the Red cut these runes. To Sigmund was Odindisa a good sister."

In conclusion, it is perhaps not out of the way to emphasise that the runic inscriptions, however

Plate 54. The Fläckebo Stone, Västmanland

strident and warlike they may be, are themselves
representative of cultural and artistic interests. The
inscriptions convey not only a feeling of loss and
grief, but also give expression, eloquent and valuable,
to the artistic aspirations of the age. They are among
the most outstanding creations of ancient Sweden's
artistic activity. The rune carvers often reveal themselves as great masters of their art, both in the visual
effects they achieve with their decoration of the

116

stone's differently-shaped surfaces and in the literary composition of the epitaph they inscribe. The inscriptions are memorial notices cut on cramped surfaces, and as such must inevitably be limited both in subject-matter and in extent. Nevertheless, it is possible to learn something from them of the capabilities of the language at that time, and with their help several conclusions concerning the early history of Swedish and Norse literature can be drawn. Despite all their limitations, they can, for example, give us some insight into the poetry which attentive audiences once heard the ancient scalds deliver. Some runic inscriptions may be regarded as fragments of that poetry itself — otherwise never recorded and now irretrievably lost. Such fragments cannot of course reflect the whole range of literature in ancient times, but we must be grateful for the reliable intimations they give us.

When, under the Church's patronage, the Latin alphabet was introduced in the Middle Ages, there was no interest in Sweden in recording the old oral literature. Like the runes themselves it lacked the support of the Church, of the book-learned men. The gulf between ancient and medieval times in Sweden was wide and deep, and oral traditions, unwritten, were not strong enough to pass over it. Unfortunately, there were in Sweden no guards mounted on the frontier, ready to intercept and save the remnants of ancient tradition before they were swept over into the land of forgetfulness and irretrievably lost. Things were better in Iceland.

Various kinds of record were undoubtedly made in the early period, but the only ones preserved are those made in material that could withstand the tooth of time — stone and metal. It is equally certain, on the other hand, that from the oldest times it was usual to cut runic records in more easily-handled material, especially wood. The preserved inscriptions can thus not be considered by any means fully representative of the use of runes in the Viking Age, in spite of the great numbers of rune stones that have survived. They give us a one-sided picture of the subject-matter that was recorded and of the general uses to which runic writing was put.

POETRY IN RUNES

Runic inscriptions in verse have been quoted at several points in the text above, and it may be appropriate here to give a brief survey of what may be learned from the rune stones about ancient Swedish poetry.

One of the most impressive of rune stone poems is the stanza about Theodric inscribed on the Rök stone (see pp. 11—15 above). It consists of an eight-lined strophe in *fornyrðislag*, the epic metre in which most of the Eddaic poems are composed. Practically all the verse preserved in our runic inscriptions is in this metre.

The subject of the Rök stone's stanza has been considered to be the famous equestrian statue of Theodric the Great, which the Emperor Charlemagne moved to Aachen in 801 from its original site in Ravenna, the place where the legend-crowned king of the Ostrogoths had resided and where his tomb was built. *Þioðrikʀ* may also be identified with Theodric, king of the Franks (511—34). My further comments on the stanza will confine themselves to some points in its diction.

The adjectival phrase, *stilliʀ flutna*, used of Theodric in the poem, will probably sound familiar to any reader of old Norse poetry; *stilliʀ* is one of the many words for 'king', well known in Eddaic and scaldic verse. The phrase *stillir lýða*, 'lord of men', is found in a verse attributed to Brage the Old, who tradition says flourished in the ninth century, at the same time, that is, as the rune master of the Rök stone; and in the Eddaic poem, *Guðrúnarkviða* III (Third Lay of Gudrun), we find *stillir herja*. (Oddly enough, it is precisely of Theodric that the phrase is used in this poem!)

The word that qualifies *stilliʀ* here is *flutnaʀ*, 'sea-warriors', and this is also a term that belongs to the language of poetry. It will be enough to refer once more to Brage the Old. He uses the word in his *Ragnarsdrápa*, where the pictures on a shield are described:

> *Þat segik fall á fǫgrum*
> *flotna randar botni*

"This I say, that the fall of sea-warriors is pictured on the beautiful shield".

Exactly the same kind of phrase as the Rök stone's *stilliʀ flutna* is used, for example, by the scald Óttarr

Svarti, who calls the "chief of the sea-warriors" *gildir flotna*.

According to the Rök stanza, Theodric *reð* ... *strandu HræiðmaraR*, 'ruled over the strand of the Reid-sea', a place-name which also belongs to the special language of poetry. — The hero-king sits *a gota sinum; goti* is a word used in poetry for 'horse'. In the last line of the verse he is called *skati Mæringa*, 'prince of the Mærings', and a parallel to this is found in the Old English poem, *Deor*, where it says:

> Þeodric ahte
> þritig wintra
> Mæringa burg:
> þæt wæs monegum cuþ.

"Theodric held / for thirty winters / the Mærings' fortress: / that was known to many." There was probably no great lapse of time between the inscription of the Rök stone and the composition of the Old English poem.

On the whole, it may be said that the rune-stone verse of Sweden, both in form and diction, is completely at home in the literary milieu which we know so well from Old Norwegian and Old Icelandic poetry. It is a happy chance that at any rate this one example of the poetry that was made in Götaland in the ninth century was recorded in runes and, thanks to the durability of the material, has been preserved to our time. And we should not forget to note, perhaps, that our record of this little Swedish poem is older by several centuries

120

than our sources for the early poetry of Norway and Iceland, which, as is well known, is mostly preserved in manuscripts from late medieval times.

As was mentioned earlier, the Rök inscription opens with some particularly impressive runes. The alliteration and solemn rhythm give an impression of highly-wrought artistic prose: *Aft Væmoð standa runaʀ þaʀ. Æn Varinn faði, faðiʀ aft faigian sunu* ("For Væmod stand these runes. And Varin wrote them, the father for his dead son").

In the text itself are also many examples of phrasing and word order that are characteristic of the poetic style. A well-known type of kenning occurs, for instance, in the sentence, with its calculated rhythmical effects, which immediately follows the Theodric stanza: *þat sagum tvalfta, hvar hæstʀ se Gunnaʀ etu vettvangi an, kunungaʀ tvaiʀ tigiʀ svað a liggia* ("That I tell as the twelfth, where the horse of Gunn [i. e. the horse of the valkyrie, the wolf] sees food on the battle-field, where twenty kings lie").

The Rök stone is of course a unique literary monument, but, as we have seen, the rune stones of the eleventh century also offer many examples of poetry, albeit of a more ordinary kind.

In this connection our interest must naturally be attracted to the signature of the rune carver at the end of the long inscription on the Hillersjö rock: *Þorbiorn skald* (p. 77 above). He is not the only rune writer to give himself the cognomen of *skald*, 'scald' or 'poet' — we know a *Grimʀ skald* in Uppland and an *Uddr skald* in Västergötland. It would be of the greatest interest to know what the poetry was like which gained this honourable title for Torbjörn, Grim and Udd.

It is necessary to remember that the word *skald* by no means had the specialised meaning which modern literary historians give to the terms, 'scald' 'scaldic poetry', and 'scaldic poem' — in English this specialised sense is sometimes conveyed by the terms, 'court poet' and 'court poetry'. The adjective 'scaldic' is now generally used as a technical term to describe types of Norse poetry that, in part because of their more intricate artistry, stand in some contrast to the simpler, more popular, and anonymous Eddaic poems. This limited sense of the word *skald* did not of course exist when the rune stones were inscribed. The word meant poet and gave no indication of what sort of verse a man composed. Thus, the appearance of the word on the rune stones is not in itself evidence that scaldic poets — in the technical sense of the term — flourished in Sweden, although there are other good grounds for believing that they did.

It is indeed evident that in their time Swedish audiences also strained respectful ears to catch the full import of the highly-wrought diction of scaldic poetry, with its involute kennings, its rich and intricate images, its strict metrical rules that governed the number of syllables in the line and the obligatory assonance and alliteration. For we know that many practitioners of this characteristic Norse art-poetry visited Sweden, where they recited their poems in the presence of kings

122

and noblemen. Icelandic tradition says that Brage the Old, the first scald, visited King Björn in Birka and made a poem in his honour — that would be at about the same time as St Ansgar visited King Björn on a different errand. Óttarr Svarti made a poem in honour of King Olaf the Swede (died *c.* 1020) and, according to Snorri, Hjalti Skeggjason and Gizurr Svarti also attended his court. Other Icelandic poets who are said to have visited this Swedish king are Hallfreðr Vandræða-skáld, Hrafn Önundarson and Gunnlaugr Ormstunga Illugason, while Olaf's son, King Anund Jakob, was eulogised by Sighvatr Þórðarson and Óttarr Svarti. Visits from Icelandic court poets continued for a surprisingly long time: Sturla Þórðarson, Snorri Sturluson's nephew, was able to compose a poem in honour of Birger Jarl (died 1266) before this aristocratic and traditional formalistic poetry finally lost all its public appeal.

The inscription on the copper box from Sigtuna, described on p. 33 above, includes a couplet in the distinguished scaldic metre called *dróttkvætt*. The name means "a metre suitable for use in poems to be recited at a prince's court". It is the special measure of the scalds. The lines on the Sigtuna box may be rendered thus:

> *Fugl vælva slæit falvan*
> *fann'k gauk a nas auka*

"The bird tore the pale thief. I saw how the corpse-cuckoo swelled".

The lines seem to be a sort of curse, designed to ward off thieves, but whatever one's views as to their interpretation, they certainly show that the noblest kind of scaldic metre was not confined to the West Norse area.

The phrase *nas gaukʀ*, 'corpse's cuckoo', is a kenning for the raven, the 'carrion-crow'. Comparable expressions are found in Icelandic scaldic verse, such as *hræva gaukr*, 'carrion's cuckoo'. That the raven should gorge on the corpse of the thief is an idea completely in harmony with the poetic imagery we have met on the Gripsholm stone (see p. 41 above) and on the Rök stone, where the 'horse of the Valkyrie' was gladdened by the corpses on the battle-field.

A fact that deserves mention is that the only complete scaldic stanza of which we possess the original — i. e. a text recorded in the Viking Age itself — is to be found on Swedish territory. This is the stanza which forms the last part of the inscription on the Karlevi stone (Öland). The stone was set up about the year 1000 in memory of a chieftain buried on the western shore of the island. The stanza reads:

> *Fólginn liggr, hinn's fylgðu*
> *— flestr vissi þat — mestar*
> *dæðir, dolga Þrúðar*
> *draugr í þeimsi haugi.*
> *Munat reið-Viðurr ráða*
> *rógstarkr í Danmarku*
> *Ændils iarmungrundar*
> *ørgrandari landi.*

Plate 55. The Karlevi Stone, Öland

"Hidden lies the man whom the greatest virtues accompanied — most men knew that — 'executor' of the goddess of battles [i. e. the warrior, lord] in this mound. A more honest battle-strong god of the wagon of the mighty ground of the sea-king [i. e. a more honest battle-strong sea-captain] shall not rule over land in Denmark."

The Karlevi stanza could serve as a model example of a scaldic poem in *dróttkvætt*. It complies with all the strict rules of the metre.

The imagery and phrasing are also completely characteristic of the scaldic style. The chieftain buried in his mound is called, for example, *dolga*

Þrúðar draugr. Draugr, 'executor', belongs to a group of words that are very often used in kennings for 'warrior, champion', and *dolg* is another well-known word in scaldic and Eddaic poetry, meaning 'battle'; Þrúðr is the name of a goddess — Thor, for example, is somewhere called *faðir Þrúðar*, 'father of Thrud'. The whole expression thus means literally 'executor of the goddess of battles' and forms a kenning for 'warrior'.

Another periphrasis, this time for 'ship's captain', is found in the words: *Ændils iarmungrundar reið-Viðurr. Ændill* is the name of a sea-king, used by the scalds in kennings for 'ship' and 'sea'; *iarmungrund* means 'mighty ground', 'wide expanse'; and 'the mighty ground of the sea-king' means simply the sea. The compound *reið-Viðurr* means 'wagon-Odin'. Now, the wagon one uses on the sea is the ship, and the Odin or god of the ship is of course its powerful commander.

The word *iarmungrund* in this kenning is interesting. The same expression for 'earth's wide surface' is found for example in *Beowulf, eormengrund*, and in the Eddaic poem, *Grímnismál*, where it says: *Huginn ok Muninn | fliúga hverian dag | iǫrmungrund yfir*. "Huginn and Muninn [Odin's ravens] fly each day over earth's wide surface." The word thus suggests a homogeneity in the early poetic language, not confined to the Norse area.

A number of inscriptions in verse form have been quoted above to illustrate various aspects of life in ancient Sweden. A translation of the inscription on

126

the Bällsta stones was quoted, for example, in connection with the discussion about the establishment of Thing-places (p. 103 above). In the original this verse reads as follows:

> *Munu æigi mærki*
> *mæiʀi verða*
> *þan Ulfs syniʀ*
> *æftiʀ gærðu,*
> *snialliʀ svæinaʀ*
> *at sinn faður.*
> *Ræistu stæina*
> *ok staf unnu*
> *ok inn mikla*
> *at iarteknum.*
> *Ok Gyriði*
> *gats at veri.*
> *Þy man i grati*
> *getit lata.*

These fourteen lines in *fornyrðislag* merit attention from several points of view, but I shall dwell only on the last four lines here. The Icelandic scholar, Jón Helgason, has suggested that the words *i grati* should be interpreted as meaning 'in a lament' (cf. the titles of poems like *Oddrúnargrátr*, *Máriugrátr* — literally, 'the weeping of Oddrun', 'the weeping of Mary'). In this there would be support for the assumption, natural enough in itself, that laments or dirges, similar to the West Norse *Eiríksmál* and Egill Skalla-Grímsson's *Sonatorrek*, were also composed in Sweden in the Viking Age. One must

127

however immediately add that we should be presuming too far if we assumed that Ulv's wife and sons could command the services of Swedish poets of the same genius as the creators of these two West Norse masterpieces. Nevertheless, we would give much to know just how this postulated *grátr* sounded, this unrecorded song of lament that was to keep Ulv's memory alive. But we must rest content with the simpler runes to his memory that are still to be read on the stones.

The last words, *þy man i grati | getit lata*, are paralleled to some extent by lines on the Nöbbele stone (Småland): *Þy mun goðs mans | um getit verða* ("Therefore the good man shall be spoken of"). But this entire inscription is in verse and consequently deserves quotation as a whole:

Hroðstæinn ok Æilifʀ,	"Rodsten and Eliv,
Aki ok Hakon	Åke and Håkon,
ræistu þæiʀ svæinaʀ	the lads have raised
æftiʀ sinn faður	after their father
kumbl kænniligt	an imposing *kuml*,
æftiʀ Kala dauðan.	after Kale dead.
Þy mun goðs mans	So shall the good man
um getit verða,	be mentioned hereafter,
með stæinn lifiʀ	as long as the stone lives
ok stafiʀ runa.	and the letters of the runes."

A whole stanza in *fornyrðislag* is found on an earth-embedded rock, inscribed with runes, at Fyrby (see p. 107 above). Another inscription similarly composed throughout in verse was on the rune stone at

Hagstugan (Södermanland), but the end of it is now damaged:

> Fiuriʀ gærðu
> at faður goðan
> dyrð drængila,
> at Domara,
> mildan orða
> ok mataʀ goðan . . .

"Four sons made, / after their noble father, / manly a memorial, / after Domare, / gentle in word / and generous with food . . ."

The inscription on the rune stones at Tjuvstigen, 'the highroad', in Södermanland, consists of twelve lines, making three half-strophes, in *fornyrðislag*:

Styrlaugʀ ok Holmbʀ	"Styrlög and Holm
stæina ræistu	raised the stones
at brøðr sina	after their brothers
brautu næsta.	by the road nearest.
Þæiʀ ændaðus	They met their end
i austrvegi,	on the eastern voyage,
Þorkell ok Styrbiorn,	Thorkel and Styrbjörn,
þiagnaʀ goðiʀ.	noble thanes.
Let Ingigæiʀʀ	Ingiger had raised
annan ræisa stæin	another stone
at syni sina,	after his sons,
syna gærði.	a visible cenotaph."

The Tjuvstigen stones were thus set up by the father and brothers of the lost voyagers *brautu næsta*, 'next to the road'. A closely similar expression is

129

used by Balle on the Ryda stone (Uppland), raised beside the main road that leads to the royal estate there:

Her mun standa	"Here shall stand
stæinn næR brautu.	the stone near the road."

Reading these inscriptions and seeing rune stones standing by the highroad bring readily to mind the words of the *Hávamál*:

> *Sialdan bautarsteinar*
> *standa brautu nær,*
> *nema reisi niðr at nið.*

"Seldom bauta-stones / stand near the road, / if kinsman does not raise them after kinsman." These same lines are also called to mind by the inscriptions on two rune stones in Småland, at Bräkentorp and Skaftarp, in both of which we are told that the memorial (*vitring þessa*) stands "at the road-junction" (*a vægamoti*).

In speaking of journeys to *Langbarðaland* (p. 48 above), I cited the Djulefors quatrain, whose lines of intricate artistry tell us that the dead man *austarla arði barði ok a Langbarða landi andaðis*. The figurative expression, "plough with the ship's prow", is found in an anonymous Icelandic poem: *Sá's af Íslandi / arði barði* ("He who from Iceland / ploughed with the prow"); and Rögnvaldr Kolsson, earl of Orkney in the twelfth century, uses the same image as the rune carver of Södermanland: *Erjum úrgu barði / út*

130

Plate 56. The Fagerlöt Rock, Södermanland

at Miklagarði ("Let us plough [*erjum*; cf. the archaic English verb, 'ear'] with wet prow / out to Micklegard").

Parallels to West Norse poetry can also be found in the half-stanza on the Fagerlöt rock (Södermanland). Here we meet the interesting expressions, *driuga orrostu*, 'to give battle', and *folks grimʀ*, 'chieftain':

Hann draug orrostu	"He waged battle
i austrvegi	on the eastern way
aðan folks grimʀ	before the fierce host-chief
falla orði.	fell perforce."

As we have seen from the passages and parallels quoted earlier, this kind of correspondence is by no means a rarity.

Reading some Swedish inscriptions we sometimes have the feeling that we have stumbled upon fragments, 'quotations', from larger poems, that are otherwise completely lost. Perhaps the best example of this is offered by the Skarpåker stone (Södermanland). After the introduction, "Gunnar raised this stone after Lydbjörn, his son", come two lines in *fornyrðislag*, cut in the so-called Hälsinge runes that were developed for practical everyday notation (see p. 79 above). The lines read:

Iarð skal rifna	"Earth shall be riven
*ok **upphiminn**.*	and the over-heaven."

(It may be noted that the alliteration here is in complete accord with the metrical rules: an initial *i*-sound like that in *iarð* (now written *j* in the Scandinavian languages and pronounced like English initial *y*) should alliterate with a vowel, preferably one of different quality, as in *upphiminn*.)

It is tempting to regard these two stray lines on the Skarpåker stone as a quotation from a Swedish poem on the 'doom of the gods' (*ragnarök*), so well known at the time the inscription was written that everyone would understand their message; a poem which a father's grief found fitting to call to mind by these two allusive lines.

The antithetic word-pair, *iarð — upphiminn*, is well known in other Germanic poetry. We find them in the *Vᵢluspá*'s famous lines on the creation of the world:

Vara sandr né sær	"There was no sand nor sea
né svalar unnir.	nor surges cold.

Iǫrð fannz æva	There was no earth
né upphiminn;	nor over-heaven;
gap var ginnunga,	a gaping void was all,
en gras hvergi.	but grass nowhere."

The word-pair is found elsewhere in the *Edda*. Odin in the *Vafþrúðnismál* asks the all-wise giant:

hvaðan iǫrð um kom	"Whence came the earth
eða upphiminn	or the over-heaven
fyrst, inn fróði iǫtunn?	first, O well-informed giant?"

In the *Þrymskviða* Thor breaks the disturbing news of the theft of his hammer:

Heyrðu nú, Loki,	"Attend now, Loke,
hvat ek nú mæli,	to what I now tell,
er eigi veit	which no one knows,
iarðar hvergi	neither on earth
né upphimins:	nor in over-heaven:
áss er stolinn hamri!	the god's hammer is stolen!"

And finally in the *Oddrúnargrátr* we read:

Iǫrð dúsaði	"The earth resounded
ok upphiminn,	and the over-heaven
þá er bani Fáfnis	when Fafner's slayer
borg um þátti.	espied the fortress."

A newly discovered inscription contains the same word-pair. On a little wooden stick, found during excavations at Ribe in Denmark, a charm against sickness (malaria) is cut. This inscription, of interest from many points of view, begins with a stanza in *fornyrðislag*; the first lines read:

Iorþ biþ ak uarþæ	"Earth I pray ward off
ok uphimæn	and over-heaven,
sol ok Santæ Maria	sun and Saint Mary
ok sialfæn Gud drottæn.	and Lord God himself."

133

The inscription on this stick from Ribe is probably from the thirteenth century, but charms of this type have very ancient roots. The same formula is found, for example, in an Old English charm from the eighth century:

eorðan ic bidde	"Earth I pray
and upheofon	and over-heaven
and þa soðan	and then hereafter
sancta Marian.	holy Mary."

(On the inscription on the Ribe stick, see E. Moltke, 'Runepindene fra Ribe', in *Nationalmuseets Arbejdsmark* 1960, pp. 122—35.)

In conveying the cataclysmic atmosphere of the doom of the gods, the poet of the *Vǫluspá* uses words at one point that bear a certain resemblance to the image in the Skarpåker inscription of the splitting of earth and heaven:

Grjótbjǫrg gnata	"Rock-cliffs crash
- - - - - - - - - -	- - - - - - - - - - - -
en himinn klofnar.	and heaven is cleft."

(On a portrayal of the last battle between the gods and the giants, see below, p. 144.)

Other stanzas that might well be considered to contain 'quotations' of this kind are those on the Rök stone (see p. 13 above), the Gripsholm stone (p. 41), and the ten verse-lines on the Högby stone (p. 67).

There is now in the porch of the church at Vallentuna a rune stone which bears an inscription of great

Plate 57. The Vallen-
tuna Stone, Uppland

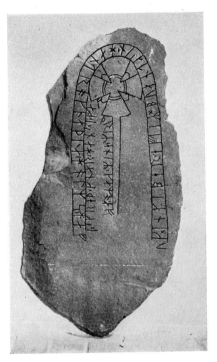

interest for literary history. It ends with the following
three lines of verse:

Hann drunknaði a Holms hafi	"He was drowned in the Holm's sea,
skræið knarr hans i kaf,	his ship sank bodily,
þriʀ æiniʀ kvamo af.	those who lived were only three."

It is the verse form which is especially noteworthy. It is unique among verse-inscriptions of
this kind by reason of its end-rhyme. This is, in

135

fact, the oldest known Swedish example of this novel metrical feature, which in the Middle Ages was to become the general rule. End-rhyme and imported metres were to replace alliteration as the basic and binding element in Swedish verse. Alliteration was indeed ousted throughout the whole Germanic world, except in Iceland where men keep faith with their traditions. It is interesting to note that the poet of the Vallentuna verse uses both modes — alliteration and end-rhyme.

In itself, after all, there is nothing surprising in the appearance of end-rhyme in a verse from the end of the eleventh century. Nearly two hundred years earlier, ringing end-rhymes had been produced under sensational circumstances in the hall of King Eric Bloodaxe in York, when Egill Skalla-Grímsson "bore Odin's mead over the Angles' land". But the three lines of the Uppland inscription represent the first Swedish attempt that we know to use this modern Continental verse form. End-rhyme occurs later in runic verses on gravestones, but runic memorials of that kind do not belong to the Viking Age, but are part of Sweden's medieval culture.

ART

Many of the runic verses quoted above form part of inscriptions which have been signed by the rune carvers. This is a remarkable fact, not least because we otherwise have to wait some centuries before any other literary works in Swedish emerge from the darkness of anonymity. Indeed, right down to the middle of the fifteenth century, all other Swedish literature in the vernacular is anonymous.

The rune writers are however not only Sweden's first authors, but also the oldest named artists. The inscriptions of the rune masters are not exclusively sources of linguistic, literary and historical interest; their work may also justly claim a place in the history of Swedish art.

Rune carvers like Åsmund Kåresson, Äskil, Fot, Livsten, Balle the Red and Öpir, created and developed the Swedish rune-stone style. Their art is essentially decorative; their feeling for proportion and linear rhythm is often superb. Their art-form represents the last offshoot from the animal ornament of the early Germanic peoples. Pictorial representation does occur on a number of stones (see p. 139 below), but for the most part these belong to monuments of a different order — the picture stones of Gotland.

These Gotland monuments, whose golden age of pictorial art was as early as the eighth century, give us rich and living illustrations of myths, legends and poems — most of which unfortunately are completely unknown to us. The subject-matter of the picture series — certainly well known in the age that created them — is hidden from us in an almost impenetrable obscurity. We have the illustrations but not the captions. (This applies equally, of course, to pictorial scenes on other ancient objects — in

Plate 58. The Picture Stone from Tängelgårda, Lärbro parish, Gotland; early 8th century

138

metal, for example — from the golden horns of Gallehus onwards.)

From the point of view of art history the Gotland picture stones are extraordinarily interesting. With their innumerable figures, their warlike men and proud horses, their ships sailing under lozenge-patterned sails over turbulent seas, they give us a unique glimpse into the picture world of the ancients. But they usually have no runic inscriptions on them, and they differ much in character from the usual rune stones. Place cannot be found for them in the present account; they deserve a chapter of their own.

As was mentioned above, pictures are not entirely lacking on the ordinary rune stones, although they are usually in a purely decorative style.

To judge from the pictures on Swedish rune stones, by far the most popular hero of legend was Sigurd, the slayer of Fafner the dragon. He is a figure introduced in several carvings that are otherwise conceived in a purely decorative way. His story is depicted in most detail and best executed on the famous rune rock at Ramsund in Södermanland, not far from Eskilstuna. Some of the most dramatic episodes in the hero's career are reproduced there — not in words, for the runic text is a 'bridge inscription' of the usual kind, but in pictures. We see Sigurd in his pit, using enormous force to thrust his broad sword, forged by Regin, through the massive trunk of the dragon's body — this forms the band in which the runes are inscribed. At the left

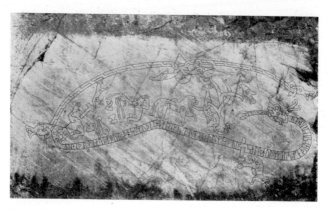

Plate 59. The Ramsund Rock, Södermanland

end of the inscribed surface lies the body of the treacherous Regin with his head cut off, and immediately to the right of him we see the smithy, with its bellows, hammer, anvil and tongs. Sigurd sits there and roasts Fafner's heart over the smithy fire. He has just burnt himself, trying the dragon's heart to see if it is properly cooked, and has stuck his sore thumb into his mouth to ease the pain: "But when the dragon's heart's blood came on his tongue, he understood the language of birds. He heard the marsh-tits twittering —", as it says in the prose accompanying the Eddaic poem *Fáfnismál*. The marsh-tits who warn Sigurd are also pictured on the Ramsund inscription; they sit in a handsomely stylised tree, to which Grane, Sigurd's horse, is also tethered.

The rune-stone pictures of Gunnar in the snake-pit, another of the great moments of climax in the

Plate 60. The Ardre Stone, Gotland

Völsung story, also introduce us to the literary background of ancient Scandinavia. The hero appears in several pictures, not only on stones, wreathed about with snakes or defending himself against them. The theme was undeniably well suited to the artists of the Viking Age, who had a deep-rooted love for patterns of entwining serpents.

The moving story of Völund the smith was also known. On one of the Ardre stones (Gotland) we see the master-craftsman, the murdered boys, and his feather-shape (pl. 60).

If Sigurd the slayer of Fafner was one of the most admired heroes of ancient legend, it was evidently Thor and stories of his adventures that were most popular of all the gods and myths. His fight with the Midgard serpent was a particularly favourite theme with poets and artists. One of the pictures on the rune stone at Altuna church (Uppland), carved by "Balle and Frösten, companions of Livsten", appears as an illustration of the old tale of Thor's great expedition to fish for the Midgard serpent. The stone was raised in memory of two men, Holmfast and his son, Arnfast, who "were both burnt in their house".

On the lower part of one side there is a picture of a man standing in a boat which has a very high stem and stern and a massive rudder. The man in the boat faces outwards towards the spectator; in his right hand he has a raised hammer, while from his left a very thick rope runs down into the water. A clumsy-looking object hangs at the other end of

Plate 61. One side of the rune stone at Altuna Church, Uppland

the rope, and must certainly be intended to represent a piece of bait of unusual size. Below and beside the bait a sea-monster is coiled. There can be no doubt but that the man in the boat is Thor, the hammer is Mjölner, the bait is the ox-head, which Thor wrenched off one of the giant Hymer's beasts, and the monster is the Midgard serpent. The agreement between the picture on the Altuna stone and the description of this episode in West Norse literary sources is very close. The story told by Snorri Sturluson in his *Edda* (*c.* 1220) may serve as an explanatory text to the picture on the Uppland rune stone inscribed some two centuries earlier: "The Midgard serpent bit at the ox-head and the hook caught in his palate. When he felt that, he started so violently that both Thor's fists went smack against the gunwale. Then Thor got angry, assumed all his godly strength, and dug in his heels so sturdily that his feet went right through the bottom of the boat and he used the sea-bed for his support." The drastic detail about Thor's legs, shoved through the ship's bottom as a result of his enormous exertion, is not omitted on the rune stone. It can be seen there how Thor's left leg has been driven half way through the planks.

There is evidence to suggest that the scene depicted on the splendid Ledberg stone in Östergötland, with its carvings on three sides, is from the Ragnarök drama. At the top of one side a huge helmeted warrior can be seen. Below the warrior a beast is tearing at his foot (pl. 62). This beast is probably the Wolf Fenrir, the brother of the Midgard serpent. If this is so, the warrior who is being attacked by the fearsome wolf must be Odin. A striking parallel to this picture is to be found on a stone cross at Kirk Andreas on the Isle of Man; Odin, armed with a spear, is being attacked there in exactly the same way by the monstrous wolf.

There are other pictures that can lead our thoughts to the world of ancient myth and poetry. Thus, on

144

Plate 62. The Ledberg Stone (back), Östergötland

one of the Hunnestad stones (Skåne) we see a witch-
woman riding on an animal — undoubtedly intended to be a wolf — and using a snake for reins.
This might serve as an illustration to accompany
the description of Hyrrokin, when the gods, finding
themselves in an embarrassing situation, summoned

Plate 63 a. The Böksta Stone, Uppland

her from the world of giants: "And when she came, she rode on a wolf and had a snake for reins" (*En er hon kom ok reið vargi ok hafði hǫggorm at taumum;* from Snorri's *Edda*). It was a wolf like this, moreover, that the Rök inscription calls 'the Valkyrie's horse', who saw food on the battlefield where the dead kings lay (see p. 14 above).

Sometimes more everyday scenes are depicted on the rune stones. The rune carver of the Böksta stone (Uppland) has given us pictures from an elk-hunt

146

Plate 63 b. The Böksta Stone; detail: the hunting skier

in winter (pl. 63a). The stone has been damaged, but the subject of the picture is quite clear. In the middle of the inscription there is a horseman with a spear in his hand, and in front of him two dogs give chase to an elk; at the extreme left a man is standing on skis, ready to let fly his arrow at the fugitive game. A large bird is depicted at the top, and another bird has struck his talons into the elk's head; these birds are undoubtedly hawks. There are two other carvings from the eleventh century that make contributions to falconry's long and interesting history.

COLOUR

In discussing the pictorial and decorative elements of the rune stones, it is not inappropriate to recall that the inscriptions were originally painted in different colours. The use of colour must have meant

147

a remarkable addition to the beauty and artistic effect of the monuments. Painting also served a practical purpose, for without colour the often intricate decoration would have been difficult to follow, and the runes themselves in most cases all too difficult to read. Once upon a time, then, the runes, the decorative motives, and the pictures were all resplendent in bright colour. That this is historical fact and not an assumption based on any *a priori* notions about the Vikings' love of rich colours has been most strikingly demonstrated by some recent runic discoveries. Some rune stones themselves, moreover, tell us that they were painted.

Of particular interest in this connection is the four-lined stanza on one of the stones at Överselö church (Södermanland):

> *Her skal standa*
> *stæinaʀ þessiʀ,*
> *runum ruðniʀ*
> *ræisti Guðlaug . . .*

"Here shall stand / these stones, / red with runes, / Gudlög raised them ..."

The expression, *stæinaʀ, runum ruðniʀ*, may be compared with the words, *stafir, ristnir ok roðnir*, in the Eddaic poem, *Guðrúnarkviða* II (Second Lay of Gudrun):

> *Vóru í horni*
> *hvers kyns stafir*
> *ristnir ok roðnir*
> *ráða ek ne máttak . . .*

"There were in the horn / all kinds of rune-letters, / cut and red-coloured, / read them I could not."

It is not only in the poems of the *Edda* that runes play an important part. The sagas of Icelanders and other Old Icelandic literature can tell us much about their use. The best-known example of a poem recorded in runes is found in a famous episode in the *Egils saga Skalla-Grímssonar*, where Egil's poem is said to have been cut on a wooden pole. This poem, the *Sonatorrek*, composed according to the saga's chronology about A.D. 960, is the most beautiful and most passionate of all scaldic poems. — Red-coloured runes decided the fate of the outlaw, Grettir the Strong: the runes, which the sorceress Þuríðr cuts and colours red with her own blood, bring about the hero's death.

Two other rune stones from Södermanland also say explicitly that they were painted. Thus, the inscription on one of the Gerstaberg stones (Ytter-järna parish) ends with the words: *Æsbiorn risti, ok Ulfʀ stæindi* ("Äsbjörn cut, and Ulv painted").

The same verb *stæina*, still alive in Icelandic (and English) with its old sense of 'to paint', appears on the Nybble stone (Överselö parish), which, as far as can be seen, appears to have been inscribed by the same Äsbjörn who signed the Gerstaberg stone:

> *Stæin hiogg Æsbiorn*
> *stæindan at vitum,*
> *bant með runum.*
> *Ræisti Gylla*
> *at Gæiʀbiorn, boanda sinn, ok Guðfriðr at faður sinn.*

149

Hann va_R boandi
bæztr i Kili.
Raði sa_R kunni.

"Äsbjörn carved the stone, / coloured as a memorial, / he bound it with runes. / Gylla raised it / after Gerbjörn, her husband, and Gudfrid after his father. / He was the best / yeoman in Kil. / Let him read who can."

Painting of the inscribed surface is possibly also referred to on the Hogrän stone (Gotland):

Hier mun standa	"Here shall stand
stainn at merki	the stone as a memorial
biartr a biargi	bright on the rock
en bro fyri_R	and the bridge in front.
Roðbiern risti	Rodbjern cut
runa_R þessi,	these runes,
Gai_Rlaif_R suma_R	Gerlev some
er garla kann.	who well knows how."

When the rune carver calls the stone *biartr a biargi*, he may well be referring not merely to the light surfaces of this magnificent monument, but also to the colours with which the runes and decoration were painted.

An original connection between painting and rune writing is also shown by the use of the verb *fa* (pret. *faði*). This verb originally meant to paint, but it is evident that even in the earliest runic inscriptions it has already acquired the more general sense of write and is more or less synonymous with

Plate 64. The Hogrän
Stone, Gotland

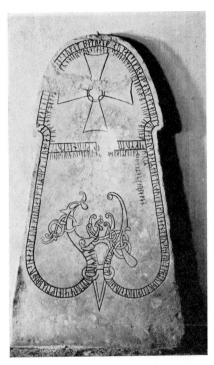

the verbs *writan* (English 'write') and *wurkian* (English 'work'), which also occur in Primitive Norse inscriptions. *Fa* (< *faihian*) is still found in a few inscriptions from the Viking Age, but as a rule it has been replaced by the verbs *haggva* ('hew'), *rista* ('cut, incise') or *marka* ('mark').

Two interesting illustrations of the custom of painting the inscribed runes can be culled from the *Hávamál*. At one point in the poem, the rune-wise Odin says:

> *svá ek ríst*
> *ok í rúnum fák*

151

("thus I cut and I colour in the runes"). And in another place these questions are asked:

Veitstu, hvé rísta skal?	"Do you know how you shall cut?
Veitstu, hvé ráða skal?	Do you know how you shall read?
Veitstu, hvé fá skal?	Do you know how you shall paint?"

The oldest direct allusion to painted runes comes, however, from a source outside the Norse sphere. I refer to the well-known line by Venantius Fortunatus in a poem written towards the end of the sixth century:

Barbara fraxineis pingatur runa tabellis.

"The runes of the barbarians are painted on boards of ash."

These literary references to the painting of runes have, of course, their own special interest, but it is impossible to find in them any detailed information about the appearance of the stones when fresh from the hands of the rune master. Fortunately, a whole series of Swedish finds can now illuminate this hitherto obscure matter.

A number of rune stones have been discovered with their original colouring still on them. These stones have come to light in places where they have been protected for many centuries from sunlight and severe changes in weather. Most of them have

152

Rune stone from Köping church, Öland

Gravestone in St Lars church (Linköping)

been, found embedded in the walls of medieval churches.

It is beyond all doubt that the commonest colours used were red (red oxide of lead) and black (soot), although paints of blue, brown and white have also left definable traces.

In some cases, at least, it is clear that stones were painted in many colours. A find made in Köping church (Öland) in 1953-4 is especially noteworthy in this connection. Some sixty larger and smaller fragments were found, and they reveal that not only were the incised lines of the inscription picked out in colour, but the intervening surfaces were also painted. This applies both to the ribbon along the edges of the stone, in which the runes are enclosed, and to the coiled traceries within the inscribed surfaces.

As for the colouring of the runic inscription itself, the Köping find shows that sometimes colours were used alternately, so that the odd words were red, for example, and the even words black. This method of indicating the division between words must have made it much easier to decipher the inscription. In one instance I have been able to demonstrate that the rune carver did not mechanically alternate his colours word by word, but used different colours for different parts of the sentence. When the subject comprised two words (*þæiʀ brøðr*), for example, the same colour was used for both, while the following predicate (*letu ræisa*), also comprising two words, had a different colour, and so on. The colouring thus served not only as an embellishment, but also as an aid to the understanding of the inscription. By painting in the runes, the writer also had an opportunity to correct any errors he might have made in the cutting. If, for example, he had contrived to cut a ᚠ-rune instead of a ᚾ-rune, he would, after noticing the mistake, cut the correct diagonal stroke over the faulty letter. The result would then be an *h* (✳), but when he came to paint the inscription, he would pick out only the correct form of the rune and his error had vanished. There is one example on an Uppland stone, where it can be shown that the end of the inscription was never cut at all, but only painted.

With stones carved in relief, it was probably most usual for the chiselled-out plane surfaces to be painted black; while the ribbon of runes and the ornamental traceries, appearing thus in relief against a black background, were either painted with red lead or a white paint or else were left in their natural stone-colour.

As an example of what a rune-inscribed gravestone from the end of the eleventh century originally looked like, an illustration is reproduced here of a stone that was found in 1957 during the restoration of St Lars (Laurence's) church in Linköping. Although the traces of the original paint were inconsiderable compared to those remaining on the Köping stones, they were still sufficient to permit an essentially authentic restoration.

We may thus conclude without any shadow of

154

doubt that people's love of colour in the Viking Age, attested as it is in so many different ways, also found rich expression on the rune stones. Painting brought out more clearly the intricate coils of the serpentine ornamentation and made the rune sequence easier to see and understand.

The rune masters of the Viking Age succeeded in their aim — to create monuments that should stand "in memory of the men, as long as menfolk live", to use the typical words of the Runby boulder (Uppland):

> Þat skal at minnum manna,
> meðan menn lifa.

RUNES IN LATER TIMES

With the end of the Viking Age, conditions of life became more cramped than formerly for the yeomen-farmers and the young men of Sweden, and the custom of raising rune stones, in the word's proper meaning, gradually died out. This does not of course mean that the use of runes came to an end. Runic writing has a long history in Sweden, a traditional practice that died hard.

Some inscriptions were described above (pp. 99—102) which illustrate the great changes in social custom entailed in the burial of the Christian in consecrated ground. The last part of the eleventh century saw the erection of rune-inscribed monuments, often of a magnificent kind, in the church cemeteries.

Plate 67. The Eskilstuna Sarcophagus

The most impressive type of monument of this kind is that of the so-called Eskilstuna sarcophagi. They received this name because interest was especially roused by the discovery of such a monument during excavations on an early church-site in Eskilstuna (in 1912).

The name is not a particularly happy one because, as it happens, most later finds of such sarcophagi have been made elsewhere in Sweden, chiefly in Östergötland. But if this fact is clearly appreciated, it is safe enough to retain the name as the general term for this important group of artistically carved monuments.

An Eskilstuna sarcophagus, then, consists of five stone slabs, two forming the sides, another forming the roof, and two more forming the gable-ends; the last are sometimes shaped like a pointed arch, sometimes gently rounded. All five slabs have carving on them, the gable-slabs usually on two sides. The runic inscriptions are frequently cut along the edges of these end-stones. It is in these tall gables of the Eskilstuna sarcophagi that the tradition of the rune stones lived on.

These sarcophagi are not coffins in the ordinary sense of the word. They were erected on top of the grave in which the corpse was laid, and were consequently never meant to contain the body of the dead man. Any suggestion that the dead were left above ground in these magnificent sarcophagi may be dismissed as unreasonable on grounds of hygiene alone.

These monuments, with their handsome rune-stone ornamentation, often carved in relief, were painted in bright colours. Their splendour must have lent the graveyard almost a festive air.

These monuments were thus placed over the grave itself, and in this they resembled the various types

Plate 68. The coffin-shaped stone in Hammarby Church, Uppland

of massive coffin-shaped stones that stood in the church cemeteries in Sweden in the early Christian period. A coffin-stone of this kind, consisting of a dressed block of red-brown sandstone, has been recently discovered (1959) built into the wall of the church at Hammarby (Uppland). Evidently it must originally have stood in the churchyard there. The runic inscription runs along the four edges of the stone and reads: "Kristin had the memorial made after her son. Let everyone who interprets the runes say prayers for Alle's soul. Sune was Alle's father."

This exhortation to say prayers for the dead man's soul is found in a number of inscriptions. It occurs for example on the Backgård stone (Bolum parish, Väster-

Plate 69. The grave monument from Vrigstad, Småland

götland): "Sven Gislarsson had this bridge made for his soul and his father's. Everyone should say a Pater noster here."

The runic inscription on the gravestone at Ukna (Småland), which most probably dates from *c.* 1300, runs: "Hic iacet Turgillus, son of Herr Gudmund Gås. Go not hence, stay and see and read your prayers for the soul of Tyrgils. Ave Maria, gratia plena, Dominus tecum. Benedicta tu in mulieribus, et benedictus fructus ventris tui. Amen. In manus tuas Domine."

The use of such prayer formulæ was widespread and long-lived. The runic inscription on an Icelandic grave-

159

stone from the fifteenth century urges everyone who reads it to pray for the "blithe soul" of the dead and to sing the "blessed verse":

> *Hver er letrið les,*
> *bið fyrir blíðri sál,*
> *syngi signað vers.*

Amongst coffin-shaped gravestones the Vrigstad monument (Småland) deserves attention. It is provided with gable-stones, but is otherwise of the same type as the Hammarby stone (see pl. 69).

The Ugglum stone (Västergötland) represents a younger type. It bears this verse-inscription:

> *Þrir liggia mænn undir þemma stene*
> *Gunnarr, Sighvatr, Hallstenn.*

"Three men lie under this stone, / Gunnar, Sigvat, Hallsten".

Like the usual type of rune stone, these monuments that have been just discussed were made and inscribed as memorials to dead kinsmen. Many other medieval runic inscriptions are extant, however, which did not serve this purpose.

It might be thought that the medieval church would not provide a congenial home for the practice of runic writing, but, in fact, there are many ecclesiastical objects that have runes on them: baptismal fonts, reliquaries, the handsome iron-work of the doors, church-porches, walls and bells. The native runic writing was clearly preferred by the unlearned to the Latin script of the "book-learned".

Plate 70. The Norra
Åsum Stone, Skåne

In some cases a runic inscription informs us as to
the builder of the church. Thus, we learn from a
rune stone who built the church at Norra Åsum

Plate 71. The rune font at Åkirkeby, Bornholm

(Skåne): "Christ, Mary's son, help those who built this church, Archbishop Absalon and Äsbjörn Mule."

Of these two men, Archbishop Absalon may be fittingly described as one of the greatest personalities in the history of medieval Scandinavia. He became archbishop of Lund in 1178, and since he bears this

Plate 72. The Norum Font, Bohuslän

title in the inscription the rune stone must clearly
have been made after this date.

By far the finest of the rune fonts is the one
at Åkirkeby, carved by the Gotlander Sigraf. This
masterpiece of the Gotland stone-mason's art is in
romanesque style and can on stylistic grounds be
dated to the twelfth century. Scenes from the life
of Christ, from the Annunciation to the Crucifixion,
are carved in relief on its eleven panels.

At the top of each panel a runic inscription indi-
cates the subject of the carving. The whole inscription is thus very long, containing over 400 runes.

A much simpler kind of font is found at Norum
(Bohuslän). One reason why it claims our attention
is that below the runic inscription, "Sven made me",
is a picture of Gunnar in the snake-pit, playing his

163

Plate 73. The Burseryd Font, Småland; second half of the 13th century. The runic inscription reads: "Arinbjörn made me. Vidkunn the priest wrote me. And here I shall stand for a while."

harp with his feet (see pl. 72). This motive, one that was extremely tenacious of survival in the pictorial art of Scandinavia, has been discussed on pp. 140—42 above.

Many medieval church-bells have runic inscriptions on them, but I shall mention only one, from Bollebygd (Västergötland), with its Latin lines:

Dat Katerina sonum
fideli populo bonum.
Hic sonus auditur,
hic mens turbata blanditur.

Even as late as the sixteenth century it was
still possible for runes to be used on some magnificent grave-slabs originally placed in cemeteries in
Gotland. The position of runes as a form of popular
script was clearly well maintained. It is against
this background that we must consider the origin
of the idea — fantastic as it seems to us — that the
Latin alphabet should be replaced by runes. This
happened when Sweden was well into modern
times, for it was in 1611 that Johannes Bureus
published his runic ABC, intended for use in schools.
It was also planned to use runes instead of Latin
characters in printed books. In this way we should
make good the harm done to us when, "as a result
of the pope's power over Christ's tender flock", the
Latin script ousted the Swedes' honourable and
worthy runes.

Evidence that knowledge of runes lived on in full
vigour can be drawn from many quarters, not least
from the so-called rune staves. These were in almost
universal use as calendars, with runes used for the
calendar-signs, dominical letters and so forth.

In certain districts runic script has survived as a
form of popular writing almost down to the present
day (Älvdalen in Dalarna), which in itself is ample
evidence of the strong hold this ancient writing

Plate 74. Rune stave from Dalarna, dated 1628

system once had on the Swedish people. On the choir-wall of a church in Öland, there was once the following rune inscription: *Tæt bør sokna-hærræn kunnæ, runær læsæ och skrivæ* ("The pastor of the parish should know how to read runes and write them"). One has the feeling that this was a demand that the people continued to make through many ages.

We Swedes often pride ourselves on the unique wealth of our runic inscriptions, but this can also give rise to reflections of a less patriotic nature. We loyally went on using the script inherited from our forefathers. We clung tenaciously to our runes, longer than any other nation. And thus, our incomparable wealth in runic inscriptions also reminds us of how incomparably slow we were — slow and as if in doubt — to join the company of civilized nations, and how reluctant we were to gather the fruits of western culture.

SELECT BIBLIOGRAPHY

Most of the runic inscriptions mentioned in this volume have been dealt with in *Sveriges runinskrifter* of the Royal Academy of Letters, History and Antiquities. In this collection of Swedish runes the following have hitherto been published: the runic inscriptions in Småland (1935—61), in Södermanland (1924—36), in Uppland (1940 ff.), in Västergötland (1940 ff.), in Öland (1900—1906) and in Östergötland (1911—1918). The publication of the rune stones in the other parts of Sweden is in preparation. The printing of Gotland's runic inscriptions has just commenced; those of Västmanland and Närke will be published within the coming year. For the southern provinces (Skåne, Halland and Blekinge) reference is, for the present, made to *Danmarks Runeindskrifter* (1941—42); the inscriptions of Bohuslän have been published in *Norges innskrifter med de yngre runer*, 5 (1960), pp. 220—230. A large number of newly discovered runic inscriptions have been published, for the most part in "Fornvännen", by the author.

With the help of the detailed references to literature which occur in the above-mentioned extensive works, and to several in the books listed below, the interested reader should be able to extend his study of the runes of Sweden. Among works of a more general character, the following may be mentioned: H. Arntz, *Handbuch der Runenkunde* (1935, 2nd ed. 1944); R. W. V. Elliot, *Runes*, (1959); O. von Friesen, *Runorna* in Nordisk kultur, vol. 6 (1933), *Runes* in Encycl. Brit. (14th ed.), vol. 19 (1929), *Runorna i Sverige* (1928), *Rö-stenen i Bohuslän och runorna i Norden under folkvandringstiden* (1924); W. Krause, *Runeninschriften im älteren Futhark* (1937); S. Lindqvist, *Gotlands Bildsteine* (1941—42); C. J. S. Marstrander, *De nordiske runeinnskrifter i eldre alfabet* 1 (1952); A. Ruprecht, *Die ausgehende Wikingerzeit im Lichte der Runeninschriften* (1958); E. Wessén, *Om vikingatidens runor* (1957), *Historiska runinskrifter* (1960). — Recent articles in connection with the material in this volume: W. Holmqvist, *Ryttaren från Möjbro* och S. B. F. Jansson, *Möjbrostenens ristning* in Fornvännen 1952; G. Høst, *Innskriften fra Gamle Ladoga* och W. Krause, *Die Runeninschrift von Alt-Ladoga* in Norsk Tidsskrift for Sprogvidenskap 19 (1960); E. Wessén, *Runstenen vid Röks kyrka* (1958); L. Jacobsen, *Rökstudier* in Arkiv för nordisk filologi 76 (1961); Jón Helgason, *Bällsta-stenarnas »i grati»* in Arkiv för nordisk filologi 59 (1944); S. B. F. Jansson, *Hammarbystenen och Hammarbykistan* in Fornvännen 1959, *Hälsingerunorna* in Hälsingerunor 1947, *Om runstensfynden vid Köping på Öland* in Fornvännen 1954, *Sörmländska runstensfynd* in Fornvännen 1948, *Törnevalla kyrkas runstenar* in Meddelande från Östergötlands och Linköpings stads museum 1960—61; A. Nordén, *Bidrag till svensk runforskning* in Antikvariska studier 1 (1943), *'Sparlösa' och 'Kälvesten', våra äldsta historiska runinskrifter* in Fornvännen 1961; M. Olsen, *Karlevi-stenen* (1957).